Dedication

This book is dedicated to all those who dared to start and have refused to let go. It is my wish that this book will inspire a turnaround in your business.

-
-
-

Order Bonus

Where I come from, we do not only say thank you with words. We do it with gifts. That is why I am giving you a FREE copy of my audiobook,

COLLABORATION FOR SUCCESS.

It highlights all the kinds of people you need to achieve personal and business success. You will also be the first to learn about my Life Collaboration Wheel©.

Use the link below to get it.

http://successpodcasts.com/life-collaboration-wheel/

Kindly leave a review after listening.

Acknowledgement

When I started writing this book in 2007, I did not imagine it would take this long to get it published. I kept updating and "stashing it away" until my friend Michael Oluwatoyin Emmanuel asked "If you do not publish the book now, how would you have revised editions of it?" He simply meant that I do not have to wait until the book is "perfect" before publishing. A number of great people made it possible to finally make the book ready for publishing. I want to say a big thank you to

1. Various audiences from many great organizations who participated at my Marketing Excellence Workshops in Lagos, Abuja and other cities. The desire to leave something that would serve as a reminder whenever I get the opportunity to speak with you inspired me to quickly publish this book.

2. All clients and students of The Learning Edge Ltd who have taught us what works and what does not in marketing and customer service. Even though we are your trainers, we also learn so much from you in the process.

3. John Eleojoh Blessing, Osayi Emokpae, Iboje Mercy and Christy Lawani for your help in editing and proofreading the book and Faith Asuelinmen for putting it all together.

4. Osaro Irorere and Olajide Olutimehin for being such fantastic friends and assistants. Your input

in my life went beyond official and made me have the time to be away for hours.

5. My Pastor, Dr. Isaiah Wealth for your exemplary life, encouragement and mentorship.

6. Lawal Babatope Alex for giving me that book in 2010. It altered many things – positively!

7. Blessing for being there as a pillar. You are the best!

8. Staff and management of The Learning Edge Ltd

9. Staff and management of Papa & Gold Group of Companies

CONTENTS

PRAISE FOR THE Z OF MARKETING 1

CONTENTS 6

HOW THIS BOOK WILL HELP YOU........................12

WHAT YOU WILL LEARN 15

INTRODUCTION 18

CHAPTER 1 21

PRE-BUSINESS MARKETING 21

WHY PRE-MARKETING IS IMPORTANT TO YOUR
BUSINESS...24
MARKETING BEFORE YOUR NEW BUSINESS STARTS
....27
MARKETING WHILE DOING YOUR BUSINESS 30

CHAPTER 2 32

UNDERSTANDING YOUR CUSTOMER 32

HOW TO KNOW IF THE CUSTOMER IS INTERESTED OR
NOT 42
QUESTIONS 43
BODY LANGUAGE 43
OTHERS 46

CHAPTER 3 47

PLANNING *YOUR* MARKETING 47

WHAT EVERY MARKETING STAFF MUST KNOW 52

CHAPTER 4...**61**

RECRUITING PEOPLE FOR MARKETING **61**

CHARACTERISTICS OF PEOPLE TO RECRUIT 63
WHAT TO TEACH YOUR NEW MARKETING STAFF69
THE CUSTOMER 70
OUR PRODUCTS/SERVICES....................................71
COMPETITION 71
THE MARKETER 72
ATTRIBUTES OF THE IDEAL MARKETER.................72

CHAPTER 5...**75**

HOW TO MOTIVATE YOUR MARKETING STAFF...75

REMUNERATION 76
VISION 77
MAKE LEADERS 78
TRAINING..79
RESPECT 79
PERSONAL RELATIONSHIP....................................80
CLARITY OF RESPONSIBILITIES.............................81
THEIR INTEREST IN YOUR INTEREST 82
FEEDBACK 82
CONSULTANCY 83
GOALS! 84
PART OWNERSHIP..84
FUTURE PLANNING..85
ENCOURAGING TEAM SPIRIT 86
REPORTS 87
STAFF PERFORMANCE JOURNAL/FILE 87
QUALITY ADVERTISEMENTS 88
GOOD CORPORATE IMAGE/IDENTITY 88
ENCOURAGE CREATIVITY, INNOVATION...............89
DEAL WITH CONFLICTS IMMEDIATELY 90
TOUCH OTHER AREAS OF THEIR LIFE 90
WORKING ENVIRONMENT AND CONDITIONS 91
RECOGNITION 92

8

INVOLVE THEM IN DECISION-MAKING 92

CHAPTER 6..**92**

MARKETING MATERIALS **92**

CHARACTERISTICS OF WINNING MATERIALS 94
PREPARING THE MATERIALS...95
KINDS OF MATERIALS..99
PRESENTATION OF FACTS 101

CHAPTER 7 ....**102**

MAKING CONTACTS **102**

FIRST IMPRESSION 102
DON'T BE AFRAID OF REJECTION 103

CHAPTER 8 ....**114**

MANAGING CONTACTS..**114**

WRITING SHORT REPORTS 116
DAILY LIST/ITINERARY 119
MAINTAIN A DATABASE OF CONTACTS 121
CONSISTENCY 122
THE POWER OF 'THANK YOU' 122
PRESENCE VS PHONE CALL 123
YOU THINK THEY WILL CALL YOU?..................................124
PERSISTENCE AND CONSISTENCY, THE BEST MARKETING
SKILLS...125
FOOLISH PERSISTENCE 129

CHAPTER 9 ....**130**

HOW TO MAKE THE CUSTOMER TO KEEP BUYING
FROM YOU **130**

EDUCATE YOUR CUSTOMERS! 130
PROMPT DELIVERY..132
SUGGEST A DELIVERY SCHEDULE.....................................133
KNOCKING ON YOUR DOOR! 133
BONANZA/DISCOUNT...134
OPTIONS 134

QUALITY 136
AVAILABILITY 136
DEVELOP A RELATIONSHIP 137
DO THE EXTRA 138
APPRECIATE THEM 138
EMPLOY THE RIGHT PEOPLE 140
KEEP YOUR STAFF MOTIVATED 141
COMFORTABLE SALES POINT 142

CHAPTER 10 ....**143**

MARKETING AND YOUR MIND **143**

THE POWER OF THE MIND 144
YOUR BRAIN 144
CONSENT 145
DO YOU FEAR MARKETING? 146
THE "I CAN DO" MENTALITY 147
TALK YOUR WAY UP 147
DETERMINE HOW YOU WANT YOUR DAY TO BE 149
LEARN TO FORGET THE BAD ON A GOOD DAY! 152
CELEBRATE! 153
WHAT DO YOU BELIEVE? 154
MAKE IT HABITUAL 155
MIND CONDITIONING 157
MIND TONICS 158
MIND POISONS 159
YES YOU CAN! WILL VERSUS ABILITY 160

CHAPTER 11 ....**162**

YOU ARE A MARKETER! **162**

WHAT THE MARKETER IN YOU HAS DONE BEFORE 164
INTERACTION 164
WROTE YOUR EXAMS 164
GOT YOU A SPOUSE 164
GOT YOU A JOB 165
GOT YOU MEMBERSHIP INTO A CLUB 166
GOT YOU A POSITION IN YOUR ORGANIZATION 166
GOT YOU INVITATION TO THAT PARTY 166

HOW TO DEVELOP THE MARKETER IN YOU 167
SMILE AT PEOPLE 167
BE POLITE TO PEOPLE...167
LEARN TO LISTEN..168
GIVE, GIVE AND GIVE 168
READ 169
KEEPING IN TOUCH 169
DRESS WELL 169
SHOW PEOPLE THAT YOU RESPECT THEM 169

CHAPTER 12 ....**170**

AVENUES FOR MARKETING **170**

CHAPTER 13 ....**176**

IS MARKETING THEORY IMPORTANT? **176**

OBSOLETE IDEAS 177
EDUCATION 178
WHY THEORY IS IMPORTANT...................................179

CHAPTER 14 ....**181**

MARKETING & SYSTEMS..**181**

WHAT ARE SYSTEMS? 182
WHY YOU NEED SYSTEMS IN MARKETING 182
THE SYSTEMS YOU NEED IN MARKETING............184
MARKETING SYSTEMS 188

CHAPTER 15 ....**193**

WHEN MARKETING DOES NOT HELP YOU **193**

NEEDS & PROBLEMS..194
METHODS 195
COMPETITION 196
PRICE..198
PACKAGING 200
DELIVERY 200
SYSTEMS 200
INADEQUATE RUNNING FUNDS..201

11

MACHINERY VS. MANPOWER 201

CHAPTER 16 ....**206**

IS YOUR BUSINESS SOCIALLY RESPONSIBLE?....206

RESPONSIBILITY TO YOUR CUSTOMERS 207
RESPONSIBILITY TO YOUR STAFF 208
RESPONSIBILITY TO THE ENVIRONMENT 209
RESPONSIBILITY TO THE COMMUNITY 209
HOW TO BE INVOLVED IN EVENTS........................213
CAUTION...214

CHAPTER 17 ....**216**

ONLINE AND MOBILE MARKETING **216**

EMAIL MARKETING 218
SOCIAL MEDIA MARKETING 227
BLOGGING 231
MOBILE MARKETING...233
WHEN THEY CALL 237

ABOUT THE AUTHOR **240**

How this book will help you

The ideas in this book are hinged on the practical experience of the author. Having been involved in marketing activities since he was 13 years old, he has discovered certain principles that will work anywhere. This book will help you if you wholeheartedly follow the principles in it:

As a small business owner or manager, you will benefit from the book if you do the following before you start reading.

1. Review the present marketing condition of your company. What is happening right now with respect to your company's ability to get and retain clients?

2. Review your marketing department. What is the structure like? Who are your key staff? What is the ratio of the *present* volume of sales to the

13

expected volume of sales? Is it less than 1 or more than? Who amongst your staff is performing and who is not?

3. Take an objective look at your key marketing staff .

4. Take a note of it all (Write it down).

5. What are the problems you are facing right now as a marketing manager or as a business manager with respect to marketing? Write it all down.

6. Carry out a thorough diagnosis of the problems you are facing right now in the business.

7. What do you want to see? How do you want things to be? What is your vision for marketing in your business? What are your expectations next year and the subsequent years? Write your expectations (or goals) for the next 5 to 7 years.

8. Write it all and start reading this book. Whenever you see an idea that proffers solution to any of the challenges you are facing in your business, write the idea by that particular challenge.

9. Mark the book. It belongs to you. Underline points that are striking to you. Make notes in the margins. Write down any new thoughts the points inspire in you.

If you are a marketing staff in a company (meaning that you are neither a manager nor a business owner), your manager is lucky to have you because you are committed to learning what will help you on the job. People like you will definitely move fast on the ladder of success.

Well as a marketing staff, you can do the following before reading:

1. Ponder on the challenges you are facing right now as an individual in your firm.
2. Think about the challenges you are facing as a group or a company.
3. What are your major challenges on the job?
4. Write them down.

5. What are the recurring challenges you keep having with your contacts or customers? Write them down.

6. Do you think you are meeting the expectations of your boss?

7. If not, why aren't you?

8. When you are reading the chapters that have to do with training marketing staff, use the information for yourself. See yourself as the boss of your personal services to your company and train yourself to become the ideal marketing personnel.

WHAT YOU WILL LEARN

This book is timely; especially now that more and more people are engaging in entrepreneurship. Statistics have shown that over 50% of small businesses fail in their first 5 years and 4 out of 5 of those that are left fail within another 4 years. The reason for this shocking "failure rate" is not far-fetched. Many people go into business without first learning the basics. They get blinded by the excitement of their "business ideas" and end up getting frustrated. One of the basics of being a successful businessperson is the mastery of marketing. Since you are not going to be the only one that will benefit from your business idea, you will need to learn how to get to the customer, make him love what you have for sale, compel him to buy it and give him an experience that will make him keep asking for more like Oliver Twist.

You are going to learn the following:
1. How customers behave
2. How to plan your marketing with respect to your customer's behaviour and needs
3. How to prepare marketing materials
4. How to recruit people to join your marketing efforts
5. How to keep them motivated
6. How to make the customer to keep coming back to buy from you
7. Who a "contact" is and how to make him a customer
8. How to handle rejection and other setbacks in marketing

9. How to remain enthused to get customers
10. There is a marketer in you
11. What to do if your marketing efforts seem not to produce any results
12. How to organize systems for your marketing
    And a whole lot more!

It is impossible for your business to remain at the level it is now after learning all the principles in this book.

Finally, let the investigator in you do his job before you implement the ideas. What works in one country may not work in another until it is given **someslight adjustment**. Don't forget to consult an expert if you are not clear with any of the ideas in this book.

If you have any questions, you are free to contact the author through the website address at the end of the book.

Introduction

"I have done everything I need to, but my business is not getting patronage. I have advertised. I have replaced all my staff. I have changed my line of business several times. I have even prayed. But nothing is improving. Maybe I should just quit."

Many business people, especially small and medium scale business owners and managers have complaints like these. They have tried and seem not to be able to get and retain customers. If you have these kinds of problems, there is no need to despair. You have the solution to the problems right in your hands now.

I was in the same shoes as you are in now. A fresh graduate from school, I knew what I wanted and went after it. I did not want to be an employee; rather, I wanted to be a businessman and an employer of labour. I knew what I could do; I had a passion for writing and publishing. I harnessed a group of dynamic young people and incorporated a company. After a while, the first edition of the magazine was published. I was full of anticipation; my business plan said that I would be a millionaire in less than 2 years. So I had hope!

But things didn't go as I planned, the magazine did not sell and my hopes collapsed very fast. I did all I *thought* I needed to do and got results that were far less than the efforts I was putting in. Soon, my team of dynamic young people backed off with various excuses. I was in debt; I was homeless; I was jobless, but I refused to quit. I kept trying to bring the business back on its feet, but there was no money. So I decided to start another business so that I could get funds to run my dream business: publishing. That was how I started Pristine Cleaners, a laundry and home cleaning business. But the business failed because I lacked running capital. When I backed out of the cleaning business, I went back to the drawing board of my publishing business and started brainstorming and reading all kinds of business books.

In my quest to get the business running, I went out and began asking vital questions. I spoke to business owners and asked them what kinds of magazines they loved to advertise in. I spoke to magazine readers and asked them what kinds of magazines they loved to read. I spoke to various people and was excited about what I learnt. It suddenly dawned on me that marketing is the oil that prevents wear and tear in business.

I restructured, got some staff on commission and stormed the streets. While talking to hundreds of business owners, persuading them to advertise in my magazine and later on reaching over 10,000 people through my other business quests, I discovered practical means of getting and keeping clients. I learnt, in a very practical way, how customers behave, why they buy and why they keep buying.

Using these principles, I have built various profitable businesses. Due to my passion for writing and sharing information with people, I have packaged all the ideas and practical experiences in this volume to help others. They are straight from the streets. Street ideas always work in street situations. Now, you too can smile (as I now do) as you apply these ideas in your business or marketing job.

Chapter 1

Pre-business Marketing

The most important part of your business is not the product, it is the marketing. This is true because your business is all about people. Some people may not agree that marketing is more important than the product but it is true. There are many great products and services in the market that are not selling the way they should. The products and services that sell the most are those that are marketed the most. In fact, marketing contributes to the quality improvement of your products and services if well managed and implemented.

When I first ventured into business, I was more interested in developing a product than in selling it. If you had asked me then, I would never have said that because I didn't realize that was exactly what I was doing.

In 2005, I told myself that there were no full colour glossy pages magazines that focus on motivation and personal development in the market. Although this was true, but expecting that people would love to buy such magazine when it hits the magazine stands was nothing but an outright assumption.

When the magazine was finally published, I got the shock of my life. I discovered – too late – that a larger percentage of the people that bought magazines preferred entertainment to personal development. Those who were interested in personal development simply sought it in books. I am not saying this as a rule since the scenario may be different depending on your country. After struggling for several months, I threw away pride and began to personally ask people what they love to see in magazines. I was shocked. No one was interested in what I was interested in. They wanted 'hot' stories on music, movies, celebrities, politicians, gossip, 'real stuff' on relationships & romance. While asking questions, I also discovered that more women bought magazines than men. That made me study the kinds of stories that may catch a lady's attention. It was not easy because this was not what I initially had in mind. But since it was what the *customers* wanted, I had to streamline my ideas to it. Insisting on sticking to my initial idea would mean having to produce only one copy of the magazine for myself alone; and that would not be business. However when I deviated from my former plan, the change I desired came - revenues from sales and advertisements soared.

Although I have stopped publishing the magazine, the things I learnt during that period have helped me successfully build other businesses. I have also used the same principles in getting tremendous results in my online marketing efforts.

I have shared this story because of the new perspective to marketing I want to introduce to you. Marketing is the relationship you develop with a customer before you commence production, while you are producing and after production. Marketing is the oil that prevents wear and tear in business. I promise that you too will find the points outlined in this book useful in building your own business.

WHY PRE-MARKETING IS IMPORTANT TO YOUR BUSINESS

It saves you from heartbreak: Marketing can save you from heartbreak. If you consider my story above, you will realize that I would have saved myself the heartbreak I suffered if I had in the first place carried out my survey before I began production.

It saves you from waste: Marketing helps you to avoid waste. You will avoid waste of time, money and other resources. Many people look for shops, buy products in wholesale, display them and sit there all day long expecting people to buy from them. This is not how to run a profitable business. Although many people get away with it, some others do not. They waste months and months waiting for people to discover their shop and start buying from them.

If they sell perishable goods, they will incur losses and plunge into debts. Hundreds of copies of the first edition of my magazine laid in my room and in storerooms of magazine distribution agencies for months before I got an idea on how to make them profitable. That was waste!

It helps you to 'see' from the customer's point of view: Marketing is all about knowing your customer. You are not in business until you start thinking from your customer's point of view. If you are marketing-conscious, you will automatically be conscious of the customer. It would indeed be difficult for a customer-conscious business to fail. Innovations in product, packaging, advertisement, and other areas of business come as a result of thinking from the customer's point of view. If you were to take a study on companies that frequently carry out innovations on their products and services you would realize that they think in this way. A very good example is Globacom Nigeria Ltd. They are a telecommunications company that provides mobile telephoning service to Nigerians. They were amongst the last to start operating mobile telephone business in Nigeria, yet they now have so many subscribers on their network because of the way they are able to put the customer first. They introduced the per-second-billing system when older operating networks all said it was impossible. These older guys were literarily 'milking' people of their hard earned money. Globacom also introduced a cheaper internet browsing rate for subscribers in addition to giving out hundreds of cars to subscribers annually.

Putting yourself in the customer's shoes can give you success beyond expectations in your business.

It promotes growth: Show me a company that is interested in marketing and I will show you a company that will experience fast growth. Marketing either brings the customer to you or takes you to the customer. The most important point is that you always meet your customers. When this happens, your database of customers will increase so much that you can comfortably expand the business. This is growth!

It helps you to 'see' the future: Business experts call this forecasting. Marketing helps you to measure how the future will be using your present performance as the parameter. It is making plans for the future based on the number of customers you have now and based on the results your marketing workers are getting right now.

MARKETING BEFORE YOUR NEW BUSINESS STARTS
Surveys

Who says that surveys are not a part of marketing? Every activity you get involved in to ensure that you are producing the right kind of product or service for the right customer who needs is marketing. A friend of mine, Blessing once started a business in collaboration with her friend Iyen. It was a food business. They wanted to cook (they are excellent cooks) and sell what they called rice and Chinese sauce. They called their business FRIENDS and all their materials (bag, food packs, handbills and sales point banner) carried this name. The packaging was excellent. They made handbills and hired a sales girl. They were so excited. Since they were still in school (both ladies were studying engineering in the university), they would sleep very late and wake up as early as 4 am. On the first day, they sold all the packs except 1 or 2. On the following day, the sales slightly dropped. Within a month, the sales had so dwindled to the point that they were making losses. Then, they quit.

When Blessing told me that they had quit, I asked her to tell me why the business started well and ended badly.

When we both took an objective look at what they had done, we discovered that it was because they did not carry out a proper survey before starting – showing that they did not start well after all. Are you itching to know why they sold almost everything on the first day? The reason is not far-fetched. They were just lucky that people wanted to experiment their Chinese sauce menu. They did not come back regularly because this kind of food is not one that a student would want to eat all the time because it was a little more expensive than what they normally get from the roadside restaurants.

We also discovered that the location was excellent. There was only one restaurant serving that whole area. Most of the students used to trek into the campus to buy food. A survey would have helped them to know that the only profitable thing they should have done was to sell the conventional rice and stew with other food options on the menu. Then they could have started introducing the Chinese food little by little. A woman started a road side restaurant in that same area a few months later and is still there today.

The importance of a survey cannot be overemphasized.

Expectation creation

Another very important reason for marketing before your business starts is to create expectations. Young inexperienced entrepreneurs always think that their ideas are peculiar to them. They therefore want the product to hit the market before doing any promotions because of fear that someone else might 'steal' their idea before the product comes out. Well, don't kid yourself. Your idea can be copied even when you already have a strong presence in the market. We are in a world where people love to copy.

Fliers, posters, TV adverts and more can aid in helping you create an expectation in people before your product gets to them. You may even want a local TV or radio presenter to interview you on the importance of the product, when it will be out and where people can buy it.

MARKETING WHILE DOING YOUR BUSINESS

This is what we are going to critically look at in the remaining part of this book. Your marketing must not be left to 'experts' alone. It must not be left to one guy or lady just because he or she studied marketing as a course in school. I have once had to choose a Microbiology graduate instead of a Marketing graduate. The fact that the latter studied the course in a university didn't make him any better than the former. Many people go to school to 'read and pass' examinations and not to learn.

As a business owner or manager, you must know the basics in marketing. This is imperative because of the fact that you should be in a position to teach your staff, measure their performance and ensure that they are earning what they are being paid.

Chapter 2

Understanding Your Customer

As we have established already, marketing is not just about products or services. It is all about the customer. You are in business because of the customer. I am going to be talking about the customer in other chapters in this book. However, this one is to help you understand – in an exclusive way – who a customer is, how he behaves, and of course, how to deal with him based on these points.

First, you would agree with me that all customers are selfish, including you as soon as you too become a customer! As a marketer, this should be your first consciousness. If you master this, you would be able to appeal to your customers' selfish nature and make them to buy from you.

Customers can act based on first sight

If there is anything such as love at first sight, you can be sure that customers can fall in love with a product just by seeing it for the first time. This is the reason many successful companies take the packaging of their product very serious. This means that you have to ensure that you produce marketing materials that will endear a prospective client to you at first sight. This is fully discussed in later chapters.

Past experience

The past experience of customers can affect their buying decisions. If the experience was one that they enjoyed, they would want more. If it was one they did not enjoy, they would need extra convincing to want to buy. Let me explain this with two examples.

Before launching my magazine's small and medium scale businesses advertisement bonanza campaign, certain fraudsters had already moved around town to collect money from people by giving them the impression that they worked with whatever magazines they were carrying around. Naturally, those who had fallen victim really found it difficult to want to do business with me. They told me that they could not trust any magazine advertising agent anymore. One of such people was the managing director of *NOBLE FURNITURES. When I told him that he could sue us if we did not meet his expectations, he replied that legal fees were expensive! He decided to do business with me only when he saw my photograph in the magazine as the publisher/editor-in-chief. Yet, he was not totally satisfied – he gave me a post-dated cheque for the time I proposed that the magazine would be out. It was difficult to convince him because of the past experiences he had had with "magazine advertising agents."

On the other hand, the managing director of SUPER CHILDHOOD – a company that sells children toys, clothes, shoes and other accessories – was very enthusiastic when I showed her the previous edition of the magazine and a copy of my proposal. She told me that she just advertised on the harvest booklet of a Catholic Church. She showed me a copy. She however said that she would be glad to advertise on my magazine since the quality was far more than what she did before. When I went back there the next time, she gave me a check, still enthusiastic. Her pleasant past experience with print advertisement made the job of convincing her very easy.

Looking at the different ways in which these people responded to me shows that customers make buying decisions based on past experience.

Emotions

Most customers, if not all, buy based on emotions. Meet a customer when he is very happy, probably after receiving very good news. He will respond to you as if you were his pal. But meet him when he is in a bad mood, and try to give your "sales talk." He may treat you as his worst nightmare.

Let's look at this in a slightly different way. If your presentation appeals to the emotions of the prospective client, he likes you immediately and may make a decision to buy from you without delay if the money is available. The managing director of one of the companies that advertised with my magazine is an example. One of the reasons I think she agreed to advertise in my magazine was because I suggested to her that she was beautiful enough to be used as a model for the advert. Although she was probably old enough to be my mum, she liked the prospect of seeing herself as a model on the pages of a magazine.

This is why most adverts you see on TV are always emotional. They want you to think that your joy (one of the emotions humans love to feel most) is dependent on their product. Have you observed that books on love – novels or self-help – sell a lot?

Let me give you another good example. I once went through a magazine in 2007 and I saw an advert by Rolls Royce. In that advert, they said something like – I can't really remember the exact words but I will paraphrase – "…there are very few of our cars around the world. It is not for every body." When I read it, anger welled up in me. Immediately I said "what do they mean it's 'not for everybody,' I am going to buy one someday." I said it with a kind of determination and vehemence that got some heat and energy surging through my veins. My friend Onaivi Dania, a personal development coach and motivational speaker, was there. He smiled and said "you know what Kingsley? That is the way they wanted you to feel and the purpose of that advert is achieved. They just got one more customer who will order for the car in the near future." Then I felt so stupid.

I'll give you yet another example. One day, I saw a billboard and these words seemed to be jumping out to me: Your Wife's Secret Affair. Though I was not married, I was almost angry and jealous as though I was married and just discovered that my wife was cheating on me! When I stopped to look closely, it was IGNIS advertising a cooker or a freezer.

Anyway, it is certain, people buy based on emotions: fear, hatred, jealousy, joy, etc. As a marketer, your job is to master how to use emotions to your advantage.

Go back to an enjoyed experience

Customers love to go back to a place where they had an experience they enjoyed. In January 2008, I was in Claypot Restaurant with my friend, Dr. Favour. When we got there, we were welcomed with a broad smile by a pretty lady. Since we just left a hotel along the same road, we told the lady that we didn't have enough cash and would want to buy food that was as cheap as possible. She immediately gave us all the options available. Instead of buying per plate as is customary, she said we could buy as we wanted. The banga soup and fufu she served us was very sweet and spicy. I was so impressed that I told Favour that the next time I was going to take someone out, it would be to this restaurant. And I did! What made me go back to the place? It was a previously enjoyed past experience.

Avoid going back to a bad experience

I already told you about people taking buying decisions based on past experiences. For example, the managing director of NEEKAYS BOUTIQUE told me that about 3 different "magazines" had collected money from her without coming back or producing any advertisement for her. She loved my proposal but reluctantly told me that she had made up her mind never do magazine adverts again. She only does TV and Radio adverts now. Many customers are like that.

They pay to get relieved

Whenever someone agrees to part with his money in exchange for a service or product, he is doing it because he expects relief. This relief could be a physical one, a psychological one, an emotional one and so on. The better you are at providing goods and services that can get customers relieved, the better response you will get from your customers.

They will do business with you if they like you

There are many people who did business with me simply because they liked me personally. The managing director and owner of a beautiful nursery, primary and secondary school is a very good example. When I first visited the school, he was not on seat. So I dropped the marketing materials and a copy of my magazine for him. When I went back for feedback, the principal told me that the director wanted me to come back the next term. I sensed that it was a dismissal and not a promise. Then I surprised myself. I told the principal that I wanted to see the director personally. Not long after, the director walked into the office. And as the principal was about telling him that I was the young man that brought "that magazine," I walked up to the director and introduced myself immediately. He looked at me and pleasantly said "You are the publisher, right?" I said "yes sir". He said "that's nice". I am sure he was surprised that someone my age was a publisher. Then he said, "I would love to be a part of what you are doing, this is how Sunny Ojeagbase (Sunny Ojeagbase is the publisher of Success Digest and Complete Sports in Nigeria) started and he is already a millionaire." He gave me the deal immediately. This is a pure example of someone agreeing to do business with you because he likes you.

They buy from impulse

Most customers buy from impulse. Your ability to trigger a strong urge in people to buy will go a long way to improve your sales. However, the people you get like this may not remain your customers if the experience they derive from your product or service is not equal or above expectation.

Some customers buy because their friends or someone they admire bought

Some customers are like this. You can take advantage of this trait by asking people who have patronized you to refer you to their friends and relatives. For instance, DOUBLE E, a big transport company agreed and paid to advertise in my magazine, I then began informing any doubter that even "DOUBLE E was my client." Since at least 90% of the residents knew the company, I got many adverts in that way.

There are many more.

As you go out every day, you will notice them. Take note and use them to your advantage next time.

HOW TO KNOW IF THE CUSTOMER IS INTERESTED OR NOT

Don't forget that we are still discussing how customers behave. You can actually know if someone will do business with you while giving your marketing sermon! They would show certain kinds of signs. It is important to know these signs so that you do not waste your time on people who are not interested in your offer. You must also understand that getting to know these and other signs go beyond saving your time. It also helps you to avoid being irritating to a prospect.

Watch out for these signs:

QUESTIONS

A customer will ask questions when he is interested. The reason for these questions could be to clarify anything he is not clear about. Another reason customers ask questions is to satisfy their subconscious inner self that they are about to make a wise buying decision. Your duty is to nudge them on with calm reassurances that would ultimately make you look like you are more interested in helping them than in having them part with their money.

The questions they may ask include but are not limited to;

1. How much is it?
2. Is it negotiable?
3. Supposing it does not work as you said?
4. Is there a warranty?
5. How does it work?
6. What is the mode of payment?
7. What are the other features?
8. When will the bonanza be over?

BODY LANGUAGE

The posture, smile or frown, 'eye language' of a prospective customer can tell you whether he is interested in your proposal or not. A good marketer would use these to know whether or not to continue investing his time on a prospect.

1. **Pout**: This person is either not interested in what you are saying or does not believe you. He probably has a past experience that was unpleasant. You need to be as convincing as possible. Show him more facts. If he is still not interested after more facts, drop your business card and leave. Don't waste your time.

2. **Listens attentively**: Most likely he is interested. The person is either a good listener or you are making sense to him. If your presentation is good, you will not lose this kind of person if he truly *needs* your product or service.

3. **Smiles and observes you in a very keen way**: If it is a member of the opposite sex, he or she probably likes you. Some people can do business with you for this reason alone.

4. **Apologetic frown or smile if his phone rings or if there is an interruption**: This person is interested – obviously! Show more facts and do it quickly.

5. **Yawns**: He is either bored or didn't rest well last night. We won't take chances so let's pitch our tent on the first option – he is bored. Make your presentation more interesting.

6. **Sighs and folds his hand on his chest**: He is impatient. Ask him if you should drop the materials and come back to talk to him next time?

7. **Shakes legs**: Impatient. Probably wants you to finish and get out of there fast. You may need to take same action as #6 above.

8. **Looks at the product or marketing material again and again**: He wants it now and seems to be thinking "I have to do something about this now."

9. **Looks at the product or marketing material and frowns**: He is plainly not interested.

OTHERS

There are more clues:

1. **Let me think about it**: If he wants to think about it, chances (over 50%) are that he is interested and wants a little more time to either check if he can afford it or if he needs it at that very time. Sometimes, 'let me think about it' can be a polite way of making you leave.

2. **Let me discuss it with my husband, wife etc**: This is same as above.

3. **Come at the end of the month**: That is either when he can afford it or when he will need it. But he wants to see you again. That is a good pointer.

4. **Take my card and call me**: He is already building trust in you and in your product. Call him at the exact time he wants.

5. **Give me your card**: He wants to call you when he thinks he is ready for your product or service. He is interested – no doubt – but customers don't always call except in Mobile and Electronic Marketing. You may still have to do the calling.

6. **I will call you when I want this product or service**: This could (over 50%) be a dismissal. He doesn't want to hurt you by saying he is not interested. On the other hand, he could be interested but broke.

Chapter 3

Planning *your* marketing

It will interest you to know that your marketing is peculiar to you. You may use my ideas but you must make *your own plans.* You are not trying to do what I did and see if it will work for you. You just have to make sure that your business works. So you will have to make plans based on your *own* business. It is said that "proper preparation prevents poor performance". This is true in marketing. The more prepared you are, the more confident you become. Your confidence has a major role to play in marketing; so plan. Confidence is directly proportional to preparation!

Objectives

What are your marketing objectives? They need to be written down. What do you want to achieve? If your objectives are not well defined, you will only succeed in carrying out a fruitless activity. According to Dr. Isaiah Wealth, "any activity that does not produce profit is not business but busyness." Objectives help to keep you focused even when almost unavoidable distractions come scrambling for your attention. Your objectives must be realistic. Don't mistake them for dreams. They must be based on how much resources and avenues you have at your disposal for the marketing campaign.

Target

One day, I was in a tailoring shop when a young man came in with a plastic basket full of products for women. He had stretch mark removal cream, hair breakage prevention cream and so on. I was the only male in that shop. There were however, about 3 ladies there. When he walked in, he simply did not see me. He said a quick 'hi' in my direction and instantly forgot about me. He was not interested in me in any way. He faced the ladies and began to give a lecture about his products. I was obviously not one of his target prospects.

Who are your targets! Your target determines what your marketing/promotional materials will look like, what language you will use and so on.

Some years ago, I introduced an advertisement bonanza for small and medium scale businesses. Instead of using a letter or a proposal as I normally do for big companies, I only designed an A4 size information sheet containing all the information I wanted to pass across. I got tremendous results as long as I restricted my attention to only small and medium scale businesses.

But later on, I decided to extend the bonanza to bigger companies. So, instead of sending just an information sheet, I did a letter. A letter is more formal. It is needed because many people are going to be involved in the decision making process in the case of bigger companies.

I got results using both the fact sheet and the letter even though they were written in different ways. While one was semi-formal, the other one was 'very formal.' Hence my target determined my language, approach, and so on. Your target needs to be well defined so that you will prepare materials that suit the class of people you want to do business with.

Customers' expectations and past experience

In preparing and planning for marketing, it is important to carry out a survey that will help to determine the expectations of the prospective client. Before setting out on vigorous marketing in my publishing company, we carried out a survey that helped us to determine people's expectations, past experiences and responses to advertisements. A client's past experience affects his buying decision in the future. During my own survey, I was made to understand that certain individuals have been going around some cities to collect people's hard earned money for advertisements in magazines which they claim to be working for and then they never show up again. This helped me know what people are going to expect when they see me or any of my staff for the first time. It also gave us an insight into what kind of questions they would ask and what kind of answers my staff and I should have for them. One of the solutions I proffered here was to accept post-dated cheques from those who had fallen victims to such fraudulent individuals before. These we cashed after fulfilling our obligations.

Study competition

If you were the only one doing your kind of business in your location, there might be no need for this. But there are competitors in every business. Therefore, one of the most essential things you need to do while preparing for marketing is to study your competitors. What incentives do your competitors give to their customers? What do their workers wear? What do they say to their would-be clients? What is their mode of delivery? What is their packaging style? Study everything you need to study about your competitors. The reason for this is to ensure that as much as possible you are able to provide something better than they can. If not, you'll have to find any area in which their weakness is your strength.

Staff training

As a manager or a business owner, you are working with a team. You have to accept responsibility for the performance of everyone that is under you. This means that you have to ensure that they are *ready*. There are basic things your workers need to be acquainted with before they go out for marketing. I do the same for my staff. I do not take them through technical sessions that may only succeed in swelling their heads and intellectual ego. Technical sessions are important but if time is precious, ride with me. I tell them certain things that help them to get the kind of results *I am getting*. (Note that one of the best ways to train your staff is for you to first-of-all go get the kind results you expect of them, even if it is once a while). I tell them to take note of the following points. More details on staff training are in chapters 4 and 5.

What every marketing staff MUST know

1. All customers are selfish: Do you doubt this? The next time you try to buy a commodity, check if you really care about the seller's profit. The truth is that all customers are more interested in purchasing something great for a price that is as low as possible. So I always teach my marketing staff that when they get to any place, they should capitalize on the selfish nature of their prospective client. This means that when they go anywhere, they should talk about the prospective client and not about their proposal! For example, when Michael walked into *BEAUTY PAVILION, a beauty plaza close to the main campus of the University of Benin, he engaged the director in a conversation and blabbed about how wonderful the place looked. And how beautiful they were making their customers look. The director became his friend. Michael told him that such places should not be left "silent." "Why not advertise with *A! Magazine to ensure that more people can get acquainted with what you do in this place?" he asked him. The guy did.

2. No one cares about your company or who you are: That is the truth. When you go to a place to talk someone into doing business with you, you don't start talking about how wonderful your company is and how many years your company has been in the industry. Don't tell them about the founder. Don't even start telling them about the product immediately. They don't care about the information. List the needs the product (or your company) can meet for them or the problems the product (or your company) can solve for them. Ensure that the problems and needs are personalized to the prospective client. If you must "preach" about your company, do it with respect to how it will be of benefit to them. For example: "A! Magazine is circulated in over 30 cities. This means that if you advertise with us, you can be sure that your advert will be seen in all these cities. That guarantees increased sales both locally and beyond." The above is better than just "A! Magazine is circulated in over 30 cities."

3. Time is precious: I train my staff to always bear in mind that people do not want to give their time to things that are not interesting. So they have learnt to make discussions with prospective clients very interesting and short. When you do this, the clients will start asking questions and then you will have an opportunity to explain more.

4. Never ask "Are you interested?" A large percentage of people I asked this question told me that they were not! It is the easy way out for any client who may love your proposal but does not want to take the responsibility that it demands. I observed that it is better to ask people who do not look very interested to think about it and reschedule.

5. Most customers make their decisions the first time and every other time you go is to get the cheque: It takes only a very good first presentation to convince a prospective client. Everyone that has ever agreed to do business with me decided the very first time. All the other times I go back is just to ensure that I get the cheque and get along with the job. Most times, if they say "let me think about it", they actually mean "let me see if I can afford it soon." The fact is that they have made the decision to patronize you but the money may not be immediately ready. Another reason they ask you to let them think about it could be to ascertain that they can trust you enough to do what you have proposed.

6. Materials don't always do the job: I have been telling my staff this since we began. Don't just hand the materials to the person and wait for him to finish reading it, hug you and give you a cheque. You have to do some talking. Let me show you an example. One Monday morning, I was in ELECTRICO LIMITED. They deal in all kinds of electronic gadgets. I dropped a copy of a previous edition of our magazine and an advert bonanza notification proposal since the managing director was not around. When I came back the following day, I met the managing director. I told her about the bonanza and explained in the best way I could. When I was through, she told me to come back on Wednesday with my team to take pictures and collect a cheque. Then she told me that I was lucky to have met her because she had already instructed her sales people to tell me that she was not interested. The materials were well written to answer any question someone may have. People have even called us just by merely seeing the materials. Yet, the materials did not get her interested. The materials either could not clear her doubts or she was not patient enough to read them.

This is why you should know that materials don't always do the job. They are complementary and serve as reminders.

Review Price

When you are launching a marketing campaign, it is always good to check if your prices can be reviewed, especially if there are competitors. I don't need to pitch a tent here. You know how pricing can affect your marketing.

Cost

How much do you intend to spend on a daily basis? One of the modus operandi of marketing is to first write a budget for it lest you spend unnecessarily. When I first started, I observed that we were spending based on how much was available and not based on a budget. Soon, I was spending too much. Even in online advertising and marketing, you are given the opportunity to choose how much you wish to spend per day (we shall fully discuss online marketing later). I had to change immediately.

Zoning

For maximum results, it is expedient that you zone the city, region or area in which you wish to market. The reason for zoning could be to 'share' the area amongst different marketing executives who may have other personnel under them. It also helps you to carry out exclusive studies on each of the 'zones.' Zoning can also help you to reduce the cost of moving around the whole country. It helps you to plan based on several factors like the way people think in a particular place, what they believe, what they like to hear, etc. For example, there are several communities in a city like Lagos, Nigeria. There are some areas where you will predominantly find Muslim communities and there are places you will find only traders. If you are sending female marketing personnel to a place like Zamfara State of Nigeria, you need to know that they will likely be required to dress like Muslims whether they are Christians, atheists or Buddhists. Zoning also helps to easily know the average size of your market in various areas of the country.

Power Dressing

"Dress the way you want to be addressed." This statement is often attributed to the late Archbishop Benson Idahosa. The way you dress can determine who will be willing to listen to you. It is always a lot safer to dress like a powerful or important person. It does not have to be something expensive. Your mode of dressing can be used to judge the quality of the products or services you are offering. I recommend that you dress corporately if you are seeing a contact for the first time. This is for the sake of getting an impressive first impression. However, other calls can be made in semi-formal dress code. Your dressing can affect your confidence. If you think you are dressed like a powerful person, you will exude the confidence of a powerful person. No shabby dressing. No sloppiness. Dress smartly. Dress powerfully!

Your gender and marketing

Many people would want to shy away from this. But your sex is a very important factor in marketing. If you think it is not, go look up some past editions of Donald Trump's The Apprentice show. Then, take a close look at some of the adverts and TV commercials that grab more attention. It is those that have a "sex appeal."

In another light, *your* sex can determine your success with certain clients. During my days on the streets, I discovered that it was easier for women to want to listen to me and patronize me than men would. I have also observed that it is easier for my top female marketing executives to get men to do business with them.

I immediately capitalized on this and went after businesses that are run by women. I got almost everyone I visited to do business with me. If you think you are better with the opposite sex in marketing, capitalize on it. If you are better with same sex, capitalize on it.

Chapter 4

Recruiting People for Marketing

Mary Kay Ash said that "people are definitely a company's greatest asset. It doesn't make any difference whether the product is cars or cosmetics. A company is only as good as the people it keeps." And I daresay a company's bank account is as good as the marketing staff it keeps! If you are a manager, a marketing supervisor, or a small business owner, one of your primary tasks may be to recruit people to work with you in the marketing department. In this chapter, we are going to take a look at how to select and train people for your marketing department.

Personally, I do not think anyone has to study marketing in school to be qualified for a marketing job. The better you understand that day to day transactions and interactions are entwined with marketing, the less you will have to look out for people who studied marketing to fill a vacancy in your marketing department. If you are very observant, you will notice the context in which we have been studying marketing in this book. Within the context of this book, *marketing is the planning, execution and control of activities that ensures that clients or customers buy and continue buying from you to get a good enough profit in as short a time as possible to keep you in business.* In other words, whenever your staff goes out to convince people to do business with you, he is doing marketing. He is not just trying to make a sale. He is marketing your company.

The kind of people going around to talk to prospects about doing business with your company matters a lot. They can either make or destroy your business. Some people can be best described as counter marketers because of the negative effect of their involvement in your business. They may be able to ensure that you are able to make a sale here and there but on the long term, they are destructive. Note that this might either be consciously or unconsciously on their part. Therefore, utmost care has to be taken in selecting candidates for your marketing team.

CHARACTERISTICS OF PEOPLE TO RECRUIT

Intelligent people: I think this is the most important attribute a marketing staff should possess. Smart people can make all the difference in your team. Whether they are carrying certificates or not does not really matter. If they are intelligent, go for them.

People who can communicate: You want to employ people who are good communicators – people who can graphically tell prospective clients about your brand without any difficulty. They should be good talkers (not necessarily talkative!). You would know them by engaging them in a conversation during the interviews.

Good-looking people: Maybe this is harsh. But the truth is that you cannot afford to have people who do not look (or know how to make themselves look) attractive in your marketing team. People who are good looking tend to have more chances at getting audience than people who look shabby. The first impression a prospective marketing staff creates on you by his or her looks is probably the same impression he or she will create on your prospective clients. And if he goes to represent your company that way, he will create that same impression. The looks of your marketing staff seem to be telling prospective customers "this is the way we and our business look."

People who can negotiate: You need people who can negotiate on your team. You should test their negotiating power and skill.

People who read: One of my favorite questions whenever I am conducting an interview for new staff is "what are the titles of the last 3 books you read?" I also ask them questions like "how many books have you read in the last six months?" These are very important questions. A person who does not read has no business being in your marketing team. Only people who commit to a lifestyle of personal development will be able to do exceptionally well in marketing (not necessarily those who read the course in school)! And it is when they do well that you do well. Note that if *you* do not read yourself, you will not be able to tell whether or not they are lying.

People with experience: This is not as important as the factors above. Experience is important but I don't think it should be made the first criterion. People function best in certain conditions than in others. Someone who has experience in marketing in a particular company may need as much orientation as someone else who does not when he gets to another company. And don't forget that life itself is marketing. Any candidate who has the attributes above but lacks experience may definitely do better than one that has experience without the attributes. And how do you rate experience? In most companies, if anybody can provide proof that he has worked somewhere else before, it will be agreed that he has experience. Does he have experience in getting results? Watch out for this kind of experience. Results!

Results-oriented people: Hire results-oriented people. Let me show you a little trick I use in finding out if people are results-oriented or not. I tell them that in our company, I am more interested in results than in activities. I will then go on to describe the job and tell them what is expected of them. When I'm through, I tell them that we like paying based on what they get done and not necessarily a salary. Then I watch them. People who are results oriented like to be the ones to determine their pay. Those who are not prefer a fixed salary just *in case* they are not able to perform. Both of them may say okay. But watch the tone.

Friendly and polite people: You need friendly and polite people. Brian Tracy says that "a person will not buy from you until he is convinced that you are a friend and acting in his or her best interest." Knowing whether a candidate is friendly during an interview may be a little difficult because of their tension and nervousness. Interviews for marketing staff therefore need not be too formal. Help the person to relax and ask him questions like "what puts you off in people?" Don't employ rude and arrogant people. Their sitting postures will help you to know them. Another way of knowing if the person is friendly and polite is to ask someone (maybe one of your other staff members posing to be visitor) to try to approach him before it becomes his turn to be interviewed. The way he responds will give you an idea.

Confident people: You need people who are confident. Information and preparation boost confidence. The fact that they are not very confident during the interview does not mean that they will not be confident on the job if they have the right information and preparation. So watch out for general confidence and not necessarily based on the interview.

Educated people: I do not mean people with plenty of certificates. I met a young man the other day and was shocked that all he had was a secondary (high) school education. He could speak English language fluently and express himself extremely well. He has been educating himself by reading books and speaking good English through association. He was also involved in network marketing with a global firm that promotes well being and wealth. This is sound education as far as I am concerned.

Ambitious people: It takes people with ambition to make beyond average things happen. People who like to live life as it comes and take whatever (they think) life offers would remain average in their performance. Ask them questions like "what will you be doing in 5 years?", "What do you think you would have achieved by then?" Their answers will show you whether they are "chance people" or not. These kinds of people think that things happen by chance. They will therefore leave their performance on the job to chance. Go-getters are those who understand that they are the architects of their lives. They depend entirely on their actions and take responsibility for their results whether the results are poor or not. These are the kind of people you need on your team.

People who love to meet people: Whenever I am recruiting new people, I always watch out for people who love to meet new people. If your marketing staff like meeting people, then they will enjoy doing the job. But if they are scared of meeting new people, they will be scared when they start working with you.

WHAT TO TEACH YOUR NEW MARKETING STAFF

You don't have to be the one to teach your staff. Do you know someone who is good in the area of managing people? He does not have to have a master's degree on Personnel Management. There are people who have these degrees who have never managed anyone in their lives. They are not even good at managing their families. Look for someone who has results in managing people and in marketing. Let him do it for you.

However, if you don't have such people around (you really should), you can do the training yourself. That is if you consider yourself a good teacher. I suggest that you train your marketing staff on the following points. Make it as interactive as possible. Better still, you could get some audio or video training tapes on the subject and listen to it as a group. Encourage them to be attentive and to take notes.

The Customer

No matter how many marketing degrees your workers have, they need to be reminded that the success of the business (and consequently their salaries!) is entirely dependent on the decisions of the customers. They need to be taught about the customer. What do customers like? Why would a customer choose one particular product over another one of the same quality and price? You may want them to suggest the characteristics of customers and write them down.

What do *your own* customers think about *your services*? Why do they keep buying from you? What complaints have you got in the past and how did you tackle them?

Our products/services

The more your people understand your products or services, the better for you. No expert can do this better than you. What problems or needs are your products/services solving or meeting respectively? Do you have testimonies from any of your clients or customers lately? Let your people know.

It is also very important to allow your people use the product and come back to tell you what they have found out about it. People are more enthusiastic about a product they have used than one they have not used. I once met a young man who sells locally made (I suspect he makes it himself) sportin waves cream. His hair was shining. As he met people on the road, he enthusiastically asked them to look at his own hair. Then he would give his sales pitch. He made instant sales.

Competition

Who are your biggest competitors? Let your people know about them and your strengths over them. In that way, they will be able to make a sale even when someone is trying to compare your products or services with that of a competitor.

The Marketer

You must teach your staff habits that ensure that they are able to get results on the job. They should know the attributes an ideal marketing staff in your company must possess to ensure productivity. Such attributes are discussed below.

ATTRIBUTES OF THE IDEAL MARKETER

You may think that this is a repetition, but it's not. Earlier on, we looked at the characteristics of the people you should employ. We said that you need friendly people, people who read, people who are intelligent, people who are good looking and so on. Right now, we want to explore the attributes of an ideal marketing staff. Your staff may not possess all the attributes below but they can start training themselves to have them (the attributes).

Promptness: An ideal marketing personnel is time conscious and is always right on schedule. He is not late to appointments.

Good listeners: An ideal marketer is a good listener. He knows how to listen to customers so that he will be able to meet their needs. Customers find it easier to like a marketer who listens than one who imposes his opinion on them while giving them little or no opportunity to speak their minds. A marketer that behaves like this may discover that people only listen to him with indifference and then tell him that they are not interested. Customers are selfish – don't forget!

Helpers: The ideal marketer is a helper. They go the extra mile in helping their clients.

Planners: Ideal marketing people plan. Someone said that he who fails to plan has planned to fail. This is true. High-ranking marketing people write down their goals before they go out to look for customers.

Reviewers: Every ideal marketing personnel reviews his activities at the end of each day. This helps him to ask questions like "why did Mr. A refuse to buy" or "why did Mr. B agree to buy?" This question and more will help him to be better prepared by the next time he goes out. If all marketing personnel did this, they will become better and better as the days roll by because the dross will gradually leave them until they become refined marketers.

Tolerance: An ideal marketing personnel has a high level of tolerance. Let's face it – some prospective customers are very rude. If a marketer decides to be rude in return, he would think that all he has lost is a sale. But that is not true. He has also lost many customers because the 'rude guy' is going to tell many of his friends that the staff of that company have very poor manners. His friends will in turn tell their friends and word can go around within a short time. Don't forget – bad news spreads fast. When I visited a small company some years ago, the receptionist didn't treat me well. She was very cold. Well, I spoke to her very nicely and gave her a message for her boss. When I came back the following day, I was amazed at her transformation. I quickly observed that she didn't really have anything against me as a person. Obviously, she behaved that way because something was bothering her. I didn't only get a deal; I saved my company from getting a wrong impression!

Courageous: It takes courageous people to be able to stand when the going gets tough. There are several examples of how I displayed courage to get deals in this book.

Chapter 5

How to Motivate your Marketing Staff

There are so many ways to get your staff enthused and keep them like that for as long as you want to. One of the greatest pursuits of man is fulfillment. He seeks it everywhere – at work, at home, from a movie, from a religion and so on. Your marketing objectives get a lot easier to achieve when you decide to give your marketing staff fulfillment on his job. I have explained some areas of staff motivation below.

Remuneration

This is probably the main reason they want to work with you in the first place. This includes salaries, commissions and other forms of financial incentives. The choice of paying a fixed salary per month or paying based on performance (commission) needs to be made after thorough consideration. I have discovered from experience that many people do not want to be paid based on commission. They prefer to know for sure, how much they are expecting from their job per month. I think this came from the "job security" mindset. I mentioned in the previous chapter of this book that even if you want to pay a fixed salary, it is wise to test if your prospective staff is afraid of being paid based on performance. Of course, many people will not like it. Their fear is founded on many "what-ifs." Nonetheless, financial reward is one of the best ways to keep your staff motivated to work.

When I became an authorized marketing agent for a company that imports GPS Car Security System, I agreed to be paid based on performance. A very good friend of mine agreed to partner with me. We decided to recruit some ladies. They only agreed to work because we promised to pay them fifty thousand naira (about $300) per month. They were very excited. It was a January so they could see a very bright year ahead. When we showed them what they needed to get done to earn the money, one stopped coming. After training them, two others dropped. Only four remained. They were ready to get the work done and get the money. Those that stopped coming stopped because they were afraid of marketing. Money is probably the first motivation you can give to your staff.

Vision
What is the vision of your company? What do you want to achieve within a certain period? What do you see in the future? Let your marketing staff see that future. And

most importantly, let them see themselves in the future you have designed. This keeps them enthused. In his book, *The 100 Absolutely Unbreakable Laws of Business Success*, Brian Tracy explained that "people may work for a paycheck, but they will perform at high levels when they are inspired by a vision of some kind." Don't just tell them your vision for the business, let it be written and made visible in the office. Let it be the screensaver on their computers. The overall vision should be broken down to manageable and attainable goals for each staff.

Make leaders

Someone once said that the best businesses have the best leaders. Don't concentrate on making followers but in making leaders out of your staff. Everyone, especially your marketing staff should be trained to be leaders if your company must have a workforce that is totally enthused. You can do this by placing them in charge of their own duties. If you are zoning your area of marketing, this is one very beautiful way you will benefit from it.

Training

Training ought to be a continuous exercise in any organization. Your new staff needs to be trained *before* they start working. When they start working, they ought to *keep learning* in order to keep their minds sharp and innovative. This can be achieved by organizing refresher courses and workshops for them, sponsoring and/or encouraging them to attend seminars in their fields. You can also maintain a library of personal development books, trade magazines, journals and audio/video programmes. Learning builds confidence. The more confident your workers are, the more they will make happen for you.

Respect

Respect is reciprocal. If you respect your marketing staff, they will be motivated to work with you. Bossing them around will make them look forward to their paycheck because that is the only motivation they get from your company. Have a policy on treating people right and with respect in your company. Everyone should be free to talk to everyone irrespective of position. I learnt this first hand while working with

World Society for the Protection of Animals (WSPA) as their Nigerian Humane Education Coordinator. I worked directly with and reported to Gill Richardson who was the Head of Humane Education in the then African Regional Office in Mombasa, Kenya. We interacted on first name basis. It is the same thing throughout WSPA. Everyone is respected. Everyone's views are considered. Little wonder they are doing so well and have a consultative status with the United Nations.

Personal Relationship
I learnt this from my friend, DrFavour. Dr. Favour, a dentist and a pastor is a great person when it comes to dealing with people. All the members he had in his unit of the church he attended were very close to him and soon, he had the largest unit in the church. He told me that if you want people to like working with you without being pushed, you have to develop a personal relationship with them.

When we became partners in business, he displayed this. Soon, all our workers were working, feeling on top of the world. I was almost jealous. He would phone them for no work or business reason, send them text messages and when he is with them, they would talk, laugh and the people won't be bored. It was amazing how they worked. So I began to do the same thing. The results were very interesting. This kind of relationship is very important so that your staff will not work with indifference. They will if they think that you see them as some piece of machinery to work for you.

Send a text message to your staff occasionally. Tell them that you appreciate having them in your company. Paying them as at when due in addition to maintaining a great personal relationship with them would do wonders!

Clarity of responsibilities

Ambiguity is synonymous with mediocrity because it is a major roadblock to the efficiency of any worker. "Your job is to ensure that we get clients" is vague. "You must ensure that clients leave here happy" is also vague. Almost every business owner says things like these to their staff. Yet, they still have problems. "You are expected to sell X units of ABC per day" is clear. "Welcome every customer with a big genuine smile and offer them a cup of cold water" is right on point.

Their interest in your interest

Let your marketing staff see a ladder in your company. Give everyone of them the impression that they can all climb the ladder of success in your company. You can do this by giving them an opportunity to be promoted if they hit certain targets in the company.

Feedback

This is another effective way of motivating your marketing staff to perform at their peak. Develop a system through which your staff can submit feedback to you from time to time. We do this at my various companies. It helps you to know where they are facing challenges. It will also help you to measure their performance and involvement.

They also need to get feedback from you. It is important that you take out time to have a meeting with them all. Show them where the company is going to (your goal/vision), let them know where it is now and let them know what is expected from them in the next few days, weeks, months, or years.

You can also ask for feedback concerning management decisions. Let them send in their views either in writing or by approaching you directly to talk. What do they think management is not doing right? As a small business owner, you alone may be the management. If you have this kind of open-door policy in your company, there will be little or no room left for "management gossip" amongst the staff. Gossip can destroy a company.

Consultancy
You are the principal consultant in your company if you are the one in charge. Allow your staff the opportunity to discuss their challenges with you. Offer free consultancy service to your marketing staff. If they do well, you will do well. You need to always invest in your own personal development. From time to time, go out there to join them on the marketing field. It will help you to know how they feel and how to handle their

specific problems. It will make you a better consultant to them. If your marketing staff always have someone to talk to, they will do better.

Goals!

We discussed how clarity of responsibilities or tasks can help the marketing staff. The next step is to assist the marketing staff to break his overall responsibilities into goals. Activities must be separated from results. The results you expect the staff to produce within a certain period of time are his goals. This is a way of motivating your staff. It gives him the opportunity to look forward to achieving something. Making each of your marketing staff to have goals would help them take the business personal. As they hit their target, they get more and more confident and motivated to take on bigger tasks.

Part ownership

Many big companies have this as part of the remuneration package they have for their staff. If you can arrange for a part ownership of your business with your marketing staff, they will go any length to make it work. It does not have to be a big one. It could just be a little percentage (as little as 0.5% depending on the size of the business). However, you will have to consult an expert before you do this.

Future planning

Why not encourage them to get involved in long term planning for the future. You may have someone you trust to make good investment judgment (maybe your stock broker) to advise them to put aside some money for investment. You may want to encourage this by putting aside special incentives for those who are investing in their future.

This will make them to begin to see you as a friend and not just a boss. If they are given the impression that you have a genuine interest in their future, they will stick with you and work more effectively.

In another light, you may want to train a certain staff (maybe as a reward of good performance) for a new position. Maybe you are planning to expend in a year's time. It will be a good opportunity to start recruiting some of your dedicated staff for the top position when the expansion finally starts. Alternatively, you may want to tell them the kind of skills you will need in the company in future and give them the opportunity to develop them on the job.

Encouraging team spirit
Your staff will do better if they work as a team. Two heads they say are better than one. It is good for each worker to know exactly what is expected of them. Sometimes, it is also good to allow a little competition into the workplace. But ultimately, it is best if your marketing personnel are working as a team. Let them know that everyone's success is important to the success of the department.

One very good way of encouraging the team spirit amongst your marketing staff is to engage them in sessions where they are given the opportunity to tell their colleagues experiences they have gathered on the streets while marketing. Also allow them to share ideas with one another.

Another way of encouraging the team spirit is to pair them whenever they go out. When they work in pairs, one person will always complement the other. Also, design incentives for the team and not just for individuals.

Reports

If your staffs are not made to submit reports every now and then, they may become redundant. You may want to use Report Forms as I did. You can design one that suits your business. A report form should be designed in way that only results can be recorded on it. In my companies, the marketing staffs are required to fill and submit a report form twice every week. Apart from the fact that report forms help you to track progress and see the challenges they face, it also helps the staff to work hard enough to have something "good enough" to be recorded on the form. Again, the monitoring system in place for analysing the reports would get a staff to work more effectively.

Staff performance journal/file

If you want to keep your staff at the level called enthused, you have to keep a staff performance journal or file so that you will be able to reward them as at when due without any doubts. Your workers will do better if they are aware that there is such a journal.

Quality Advertisements
We don't need to overemphasize this, do we? Quality adverts on TV, radio or any of the available media will definitely motivate your staff. If you are running a business that cannot yet afford this, you can do social media advertising. You can budget as low as $10 per day. More details are in a latter chapter.

Good corporate image/identity
If you develop a good corporate image for your company, your staff will be proud to represent you outside. I observed that some banks have this advantage over others in Nigeria. The marketing personnel of banks that are more concerned about their corporate image are always more confident.

Offer more to customers/clients, sponsor a local charity or event, award a scholarship etc. Boost your image in the eyes of the local public. More ideas for corporate social responsibility are in chapter 16.

Encourage creativity, innovation

Every company should have a book somewhere in the office that staff can write suggestions and ideas. If your company can afford internet services, maybe be an email should be dedicated for suggestions. If you think a suggestion box will be more effective, it is up to you. Just ensure that you are getting feedback on creative and innovative ideas. Whenever you get an idea from a member of staff, assemble everyone and praise the person. After praising such a person, act on the idea immediately or ask the person to expatiate on it. You may want to give the person a little allowance to carry out a research on the subject.

If you encourage creativity and innovation, you will be so amazed at the results because you will no more be the only one doing the thinking. Moreover, one simple idea from the person you think is the dumbest amongst your staff could just turn the fortunes of your business for good.

Deal with conflicts immediately

Conflicts must occur in the workplace. It could be between someone in the management team and someone in a lower rank. It could be between any two or more people. Whenever there is a conflict, it is always important to reason with both parties objectively. The importance of dealing with conflicts very fast cannot be overemphasized. It helps to prevent the reoccurrence of future misunderstandings. It is important to have a strict policy on intra-organizational conflict. Hear both sides and get them reconciled immediately. You may do this by taking both of them out, probably to a nearby eatery or anywhere outside the office.

Touch other areas of their life

The more of the other areas you touch in the life of your marketing staff the more loyal they will be to you. Here are a few examples

Marital – sponsor a relationship seminar, books & free counseling

Recreational – have once a month game – maybe golf, scrabble, whatever – together Housing – have a programme of securing low cost accommodation

Of course these should be done within the limits of your budget.

Working environment and conditions

Your work environment will not only determine if customers will come or not, it can also affect your staff. Bank marketers do better than the average marketers not because they are better, but because the working conditions are almost perfect. They go around town in air-conditioned cars. Apart from the fact that it helps them to work faster, it also helps them to remain neat, composed and unstressed compared to other marketers who have contrary working conditions.

As a small or medium business owner, you may not afford a car for your marketers. But they should be provided with transportation. What they put on is also a very powerful motivation factor. You can plan all these based on your budget but make it the best your budget can afford. You are not in business without marketing.

Recognition
Openly reward and recognize performers. This would not only encourage them, it would motivate others.

Involve them in decision-making
Allow them to participate in decision making in the organization. I do this by asking everyone for ideas. Then, we would all objectively analyse the best ideas and arrive at a decision. This would give them a sense of ownership. People normally protect what they own. Right?

Chapter 6

Marketing Materials

Marketing materials include fliers, proposals, sales letters/reports, information brochures, demonstration samples and so on. You must put the following into consideration when preparing materials for the purpose of marketing.

1. All customers are selfish, including you!

Your materials should contain information that demonstrates an absolute understanding of the prospective clients' needs and problems and prove that your products or services can meet these needs and solve the problems.

2. No one actually cares about your company

Your material must not contain *irrelevant details* about your company and product. The details become irrelevant to the client when it does not include him in the picture. Your material should portray how a particular strength your company possesses will make him better if he does business with you. Therefore don't give him details that will make him ask "So what?" while reading your material.

3. There is no time. People are 'busier' than ever

Your materials must be precise, and they must go straight to the point. If your marketing material is too lengthy, you may not be able to get people to read them when you want them to. Many people will tell themselves that they will read it 'later' and end up not reading them at all. And of course, your purpose will be defeated in that way. The best materials are those your customers can read immediately and start asking you questions.

4. It takes the "extra" to make people embrace a new concept

What "extra" do you have in the package you are proposing in your material? It could be something other companies are not offering their customers. Let them see the "extra" at a glance.

Characteristics of winning materials

1. They are straight to the point
2. They make the customer see only their interest. Banks are very good at this. They make you to see only your interest when they want to convince you to open an account with them or get a loan from them. "Terms & Conditions Apply" is always written in faint letters!

3. They are attractive. After taking the pains to design a material, you must ensure that it has features that will guarantee that its contents are read.

4. They provide *needed*information. Your material should only contain information that is relevant to the prospective customer, at least at the moment of engagement.

5. The information on winning materials is never assumptions. If your material claims that the robot you have for sale can wash clothes, you better be sure it can!

Preparing the materials

Having put the above into consideration, utmost care must be taken in preparing the material to ensure that the right message is passed across to prospective customers. The information must not be distorted by wrong use of language. It must not be made difficult to understand by using too much grammar. It must be concise (straight to the point). Taking the following steps one after the other will ensure that you are able to get winning materials.

1. **Write. Pour your heart**: What do you want to offer your client? What do you have for him? Write everything down. Don't try to edit at this point. Don't try to check if what you are writing is correlating or if the thoughts are concurrent. Just write. If you remember or get words for D before A, B and C, write it in that order. Don't interrupt your thoughts. Just write – fully express your thoughts until you think you have completely transferred the entire idea. You may either use a paper for this or type directly onto your computer. If you are typing directly onto your computer, your word processor will definitely underline some wrongly spelt words, and sentences that are not well constructed. Don't worry about these. Just keep writing everything out – all the details. Even if you are doing a flier and it's as though what you have written so far is almost as long as an article, keep writing what you want your prospective customers to know.

2. **Strike out unimportant details**: After writing everything you think is important, strike out the details

that are not good enough in facilitating a sale. This reduces what you have written so far to only very important items.

3. **Edit for errors**: Edit the material for errors. Check your language and make sure one thought seamlessly "flows" into the next one. Check for typographical errors. Check your sentence style and structure. Remember that certain errors are "unpardonable" as they can distort the information your prospect should get about your company or products.

4. **Strike out more unimportant details**. If you still have to reduce what you've got by now, strike out points that are not too important once more.

5. **Delete repetitions**: Watch out for repetitions and delete them. Although repetitions sometimes help to emphasize points, they can put people off if they are not systematically placed on the material.

6. **Indicate areas of emphasis**: What do you want to emphasize in the material you are preparing? Underline them. What do you want to express in larger fonts?

7. **Type and proofread**: If you used a paper for writing, type the work and proofread. You will need to give it to someone else to read before you finally send it to your graphics designer.

8. **Graphics design**: A graphics designer is very important because he is the one that will determine if people will be interested in reading what you have written or not. Don't allow just anyone to design your material. Let a professional do it. Ask various graphics designers to show you what they have done before, with proof. Pick the best.

9. **Printing**: What quality of paper are you using? What colours did you choose? Note that there are some papers that will not be appropriate if you are targeting a certain class of the population. Don't use a printing press that does not have good samples of what you want

to print. You cannot afford the luxury of substandard marketing materials. A good graphics person should know which printing press can deliver the quality you desire.

Kinds of materials

Fliers: Your fliers do not have to contain all the details of your products or services. It should be written in a manner that it contains only the most important points you want your prospects to see. Your fliers should contain as little (but very important and catchy) information as possible. It should also carry all your contact details (phone numbers, address, email and website). However, your contact details should be written in smaller fonts compared to the font size used in the main body of the flier. A diagram or photograph would make it look more illustrative and attractive.

Posters: Your poster must be very catchy. It should contain as few words as possible. It should however contain picture(s) that give people an understanding of your message at a glance. However, it is not a rule that the picture should always depict the information on the poster. It can be the picture of a model. If the model is well known, fine. But using the photograph of any attractive person would be great if you cannot afford a known model. It is always important to put the most exciting part of your poster in large fonts because people do not always stand to read a poster unless they find it very interesting.

Factsheets: A factsheet is like a one paged newsletter. It gives you the opportunity to write as much as you'd like to. Apart from telling the prospective client about your product, a factsheet can also contain other details such as its features and other products you have for sale. You may also want to tell the client how to differentiate between the original and counterfeits (if they exist). You may also want to include the benefits of using the product or service in details.

Business Card: This is a very powerful material for marketing. Many people make business cards that have their names, business names and contact details and exclude details of what they do. It is important that you put the details of what you do on the card. If a good graphics designer works on it, it won't be clumsy. If you have to print on both sides to get the details on it, do it.

Banners: If you live in a place like Lagos, Nigeria, where the pasting of posters is illegal, banners would do just fine. The fewer the words, the better. Your contact information, preferably a phone number, should be conspicuously printed on the banner.

Presentation of facts

Some people love to present information in such a way that they start from the *least* important (or interesting) points to the *most* important points. This is good if the prospective customer has the time and patience to read *ALL* the facts presented. However, it is always important to 'catch' the customer at their first glance. It could be a word or a phrase or a sentence that is so attention-grabbing to make the prospect want to read further.

Chapter 7

Making Contacts

Approaching people for the first time with your offer is perhaps the most difficult part of marketing. You have different tasks before you when you meet people for the first time. Firstly, you need to convince them that you are genuine. Secondly, you need to convince them that they need your offer. Thirdly, you need to convince them that you are rightly positioned to meet their needs (with your goods or services) better than your competitors.

First Impression
Your first impression on them matters a lot. It goes a long way to determine if the people will think you are genuine or not. The *way* you make claims about your products or services will contribute to what they will make of you. Your looks are also very important. Before you open your mouth to speak, your prospect has already given himself an idea of the kind of person

you are. Don't forget that looks can be deceptive. Therefore, you have to do as much as you can to look the way you want your prospective client to think of you.

What are you offering them? What is your mode of presentation? What are you telling them? When you visit a prospect for the first time, don't just go on telling them about your company, products or services. They don't really care about your products or services unless there is an indication that what you are offering can either solve their problems or meet their needs.

Don't be Afraid of Rejection

There are certain kinds of clients you will never get if you are afraid of rejection. One thing you need to have at the back of your mind about is that there are different kinds of people. Some people are very warm while others can be extremely cold. Some people are very polite whether they are meeting you for the first time or not, while others are very saucy. A good marketer must never take people's wrong remarks personally. You must learn to be an "insult-proof" person. You will need to strengthen your patience.

A 'No' is not a knockout

Jack* is my friend and member of the editorial crew of a magazine I published. One day, he went to B's Confectionaries, a company that operates both a restaurant and a shop for celebration cakes. His intention was to offer our advert bonanza to them. He met a pretty but not-too-nice young lady there. He told her why he was there and asked her to direct him to the manager's office.

"I am the manager," she said curtly. "We are not interested." I know Jack to be a very jovial person. He tried to win her to his side because something told him that she was *not* the manager – she was just being adamant. After various attempts, Jack gave up and left.

The following day, unknown to me that someone from my company had been there, I walked into the same office. I met a plump lady, an albino. I liked her immediately. She spoke very nicely to me. She was about twenty years old, but I referred to her as madam and she liked it. When I told her why I was there and requested to see the manager, she asked me to sit and went in to call her eldest sister. We discussed and sealed the deal. They paid the following day.

Jack did not believe his ears when I told him how easy it was to do business with the ladies. The three of them ran the business for their dad (who was on a trip overseas). As a result of that, any of them could claim to be the manager. However, the eldest sister had the final say. Although, I later met the one Jack encountered but I was glad that I had met the plump lady.

The 'no' Jack got deprived him of getting his commission, but it did not stop the company from getting the patronage. A 'no' is not a knockout!

A 'No' could be a 'call next time'

This is true. I don't ever leave someone's office with a 'no'. Whenever someone tells you that they are not interested in your offer or in doing business with you, ask them when you should call back. The reason for this is that the person could have said no because they are broke at that moment, do not think they need your offer yet, or for some other reasons. If the person is broke (which is often the case), they will be glad to ask you to come back at the time they expect to be financially ready.

Notice and Comment

There is power in a nice not-very-flattering remark. EE Leathers is a boutique in Airport Road, Benin City. They sell only leather products, from shoes to bags and to belts for women. When I first walked into the boutique, I could smell leather. I politely said "Wow! I can smell leather" and I began to admiringly touch some shoes and bags. A salesman came to me smiling and then explained that they import all their products. I told him I have noticed that already. By the time I mentioned why I was there, he had already become my friend. He did not hesitate to give me his boss' business card so I could call her and arrange an appointment.

Smile/politeness

My remark would not have made any impact if I did not garnish it with a smile and genuine politeness. I have trained myself to always be in the best possible mood whenever I walk into a place to convince people to do business with me. You wouldn't know if I was moody before I entered. You need to train yourself and those who work with you not to allow their bad mood to reflect in their marketing.

A marketing executive needs to be a happy person. At least have that impression on your clients. Smiles and moods can be contagious. If you walk into a place for marketing, there could be someone who you most likely would have done business with, but will end up not doing because he is in a bad mood. Your good mood can get the person to feel better.

If he says no in a bad mood, come back again.

Yes. If someone ever tells you 'no' and you notice he is in a bad mood, go and check him next time. F2F African Kitchen is an ultra-modern restaurant in Lagos Island. The Managing Director indicated interest in doing business with me the first time we met. When I called her a few days later, she answered roughly telling me that she has so much on her mind right now and would not be able to do anything with me anymore. I noticed that she was under some kind of pressure. Few days later, I went to see her. She welcomed me politely and tendered an apology for her unladylike behaviour on the phone. And we went ahead with the business!

Meet the Decision Maker

Members of my team have heard me say this many times. When you visit a company, especially if it is a small or medium scale one, your most important job is to ensure that you are able to see the decision maker. Don't be afraid to tell them who you want to see
- the manager or the managing director. You save time, money and energy if you are able to see the decision maker one-on-one, the first time. But note that in some

organizations, the decision maker is necessarily not a high ranking officer.

Bottle Necks

In your quest to see the decision maker in any establishment, you will always encounter 'bottlenecks'. I used to have a wonderful personal secretary/receptionist called Tom. He did his job so well that I could not help but make him a friend too. He knew when to allow people to see me and when not to. On some occasions, he went too far for my liking. I remember one instance vividly. I gave some people appointments to see me that morning. When I finished my breakfast around 10.00am (I have breakfast in the office because I always get to work even before the cleaners!), I checked the time and hissed, wondering why some people could not just keep to appointments. Then I strode to the reception and met Tom doing some typing. I told him that I was expecting some people and casually asked if he had seen anyone. To my greatest surprise, he told me that they had come and he asked them to come back at midday to see me.

As you can see, I didn't ask him to do this. I was upset because that would keep me in the office till 12.00 noon. Hence, I had to adjust my schedule for the day. There are many Toms in almost all establishments out there. Some may tell you that the decision maker is not around at all and refuse to tell you when he will be around. Others will want to feel important by trying to mediate between you and their boss. They want you to tell them exactly why you have come to their company so that they can pass the message to the decision maker and then get his reply to you. From experience, I have discovered that most (99%) of these bottlenecks will distort your message. Note that they do not distort your message on purpose. They do so because they are not as informed as you are. They leave the decision maker with so much doubts. Clearing all forms of doubts about your goods or services is your job and not this person's. Even if they do not distort the information, they cannot pass the information across with the kind of enthusiasm you would employ.

How do you handle bottlenecks then? It depends on the person.

Rival Bottlenecks: Some bottlenecks are merely rivals. They don't want anything or information to come between them and their boss. They always want to know why you want to see their Oga (Oga is master or boss in Nigerian Pidgin) or madam. If the marketer is a young lady for example and wants to see Oga, she should expect that the bottleneck will be narrower if the receptionist is a young lady that likes her boss. She will ask questions like 'why do you want to see him?', 'what's his name?', 'is he expecting you?' etc. If you meet this kind of bottleneck, do your best not to be seen as a threat. Be nice!

NOTE: You may want to ask 'why this emphasis on bottlenecks?' The fact is that someone you regard as a 'common security guard' can either assist or prevent you from winning a business you otherwise should get. If they do not allow you or your proposal to get to the appropriate person, that is it. So, it pays to take them very, VERY serious.

InquisitiveBottlenecks: An inquisitive bottleneck wants to KNOW for sure, why you want to see his boss. He wants you to give him all the details whether you want to or not. If you do not give him all the details, he may not want to allow you to see his boss. So how do you handle him? Humour him! Tell him everything, if you can, and he will allow you to see his boss. However, you have to be careful because if he thinks that his (employer) company does not need your service, he may not allow you to see the decision maker.

Mediator Bottlenecks: These types of bottlenecks do not want you to see their boss. They just want you to tell them whatever you want to tell their boss. They want to act as mediators. How do you deal with this? There are two ways you can deal with this kind of situation. You either allow them to mediate between you and their boss or get to see their boss 'your own way.'

If you want the overzealous individual to act as a mediator between you and his boss, simply sit him down and then give him a thorough 'lecture' on why his company or organization should do business with you. Let the enthusiasm you will express in the presence of this individual be the same as the one you will give his boss. Let your presentation be interactive. Ensure that he is getting your message by studying his body language. Make him like you. Make him feel very important. Then take his phone number and call him the moment you get to your office or home. Sometimes, a good mediator who likes you will do wonders for you.

On the other hand, you may want to fight your way through to the decision maker. This is not a physical combat or a fight of words. It is very easy. Simply make the person to like you. You can even go as far as giving him a lecture as though you want him to actually discuss with his boss on your behalf. Then ask for their business cards or fliers. Check their sign post or banner (if any). You will find some phone numbers on these materials. Ask the bottleneck to underline his number amongst the numbers. The other numbers (or at least one of them) may likely be the decision maker's.

Not all bottlenecks are bottlenecks!

There are people who you think are bottlenecks, but are not, as a matter of fact. They may even be mere sales boys or girls in an organization who have the ability to take decisions on behalf of the owner of the business. The reason for this could be that the owner of the business is not in the country. So, you will agree with me that some supposed bottlenecks are actually decision makers.

Chapter 8

Managing Contacts

The person who has agreed to do business with you - by promising a date or by agreeing to discuss the prospect with their partners or colleague – is your contact. He is so regarded because of the keen interest shown and the willingness to write you a cheque as soon as possible. What should interest you more than anything else is the number of contacts or people that are ready to pay for your goods or services at the end of the day and not the ones you actually met. If the people ended up not paying, you are merely carrying out 'activities.' My team members have heard me say over and over again that,

"We are in business for results and not for activities. You are paid for results and not for the activities you get involved in". They are fully aware that I am more impressed with a short list of paying contacts than a long list of visiting prospects.

It is generally said that anything well-managed will grow. Hence, get your contacts, especially the paying ones, and then make it your primary responsibility to manage them well. Managing your contacts is simply doing those things (and making them do things) that will make your contacts have you and your proposal in mind. Your job of managing contacts entails not just calling to remind them that they have agreed to do business with you but doing at least a single thing per day that will ensure that they metamorphose from being just contacts to becoming '*paying clients*.' You can make this happen by consistently doing the following.

Writing short reports
This is the first step in managing your contacts. The daily reports you write will help you to remember the following:

1. When next to visit a contact;
2. What to say to him when next you visit; (it is always important to start your conversation with 'last time, you said…' It enables the contact to remember his commitment to you. It would also give the contact an impression that you are an effective person and you know what the right impressions can make happen! and
3. What materials you should take along as you go visiting.

The daily report does not have to be written like an essay. It does not have to be on an A4 writing pad. It could be written on a jotter. And you don't need to write much. This is to ensure that you are able to read it at any time in just half a minute per contact. Apart from the one in writing pad, create a table on MS Excel to keep all the data. Your reports should be updated every time you make 'contact with your contacts.' That is a funny expression, right?

Personally, I used to go out with a small jotter in my back pocket. Each leaf in the jotter is one quarter of an A4 paper. When I meet a promising contact who I know will be a paying client, I write his name (or in some cases, the name of his business), his phone number and a summary of what he said. I also include the date of our next meeting. If there is anything he wants me to come along with in my next call, I also write it down. All these can be written in a space that is not more than one-fifth of the jotting space. This is a very effective and time-saving way of writing reports on the go. All my staff have such jotters. They know that I do not have the time and patience for essay-like reports. However, if your boss is more interested in an essay-like report, give it to him. We all have different values. Below are typical examples of the kind of on-the-go reports we write in my companies. These ones are drawn directly from my jotter.

Mr. B's. MD – 0802*******.Very interested. Thursday 25th 4pm. Come with sample design.

Apart from the fact that it was very easy for me to take down the above information while in touch with the contact, it also helped me to know the exact time I was supposed to go back to see him, at a glance. I also knew what to take with me when I am going back to see him.

It will interest you to know that there is no 'not interested' in my jotter. If someone is not interested, I have no reason to write his name in my jotter. He is definitely not a contact. s

Let me show you another example.

GPG Ltd. Manager interested. Dropped proposal for MD. Check by 1pm or 2pm tomorrow.

Note that 'dropped proposal for MD' above means the MD (managing director) was not in the office on my arrival. I was asked to check back by 1 or 2pm the next day as the manager thought the MD would most likely be on seat then.

I am not yet sure if this contact will do business with me because no matter how much my offer excites the manager, it is still the Managing Director that will decide whether the company will do business with me or not. If the MD agrees, their company remains on my contact list. But if not, I will strike what I wrote about them with a pen and they would never make it to my excel sheet.

Daily list/itinerary

Your daily itinerary is very important if you want to have some people pay as soon as possible. It is helpful to have a list of the places you hope to visit on a day. Personally, I prepare this list the evening before the next business day. Preparing it the evening before the day enables me to have an idea of how the next day will go and I can save time for other activities. Also, it prevents time wastage with just one contact (it is very easy for some contacts to keep you around them especially if they like your personality. It happens to me a lot. Your list will keep you closely in touch and on track always.

Also be sure to always take a look at the list from time to time to measure your progress. Tick any one you have seen or called. You do not have to write them in the order in which you want to see them. Below is a typical example for me:

FRIDAY

XYZ Concepts

City Frost

Johnterner Ltd (3pm)

Play VRoom

15 Wine Ltd

Mascaras Concept

Photostope

Michaels Boutique

I wrote 3.00pm by Johnterner Ltd because the owner told me specifically that 3.00pm is the only time I will get him in the office. Others can be seen at any time I get to their places of business. Also note that most of these businesses are in the same area. If I decide to visit businesses without a plan, I will end up going to almost every area in the city. This is both time and money consuming. If you live and work in a city that is as busy and large as mine (Lagos), you wouldn't want to run the length and breadth of the city to see just a handful of contacts.

Maintain a database of contacts

One of the most important parameters in managing your contacts is to maintain a database of contacts. Whenever you engage in marketing, the people you will be talking to will either be interested in your goods or services or not. Some will tell you that they will be ready next month, next quarter, or next year. Note these in your jotter and transfer them into a Notebook or MS Excel on your computer. Then visit them the moment the time they promised starts drawing close. In maintaining a database of contacts, you need to have their phone numbers and details of what they said. Did any one tell you that he will relocate soon? You should have an idea of which part of the city he is going to.

Consistency

When you call your contacts, you should be able to remember exactly what they said the last time you met or discussed. This alone will make them to conclude that you:

1. care about them or their business to the point that you remembered the last conversation you had with them;
2. are a responsible person; and
3. work for a responsible organization

The power of 'Thank You'

The phrase 'thank you' is very powerful. I experienced it first-hand when I did business with XY Wines and Spirits Company. After several follow-ups on a particular deal, they gave me a handsome cheque which I happily took to my bank to pay in. The following Tuesday, I went to the company again. I met the

Managing Director and thanked him for doing business with me. Guess what he did. He brought a business card out of his pocket and wrote "Bearer is from me. Please listen to him." He signed it and told me to go to the General Manager of a very big company. That was a big referral. Learn to say 'thank you' to your client after a fruitful deal. It can work miracles.

Presence Vs Phone Call

Sometimes, it is good to call your contacts, especially if they are far away. This call is not meant to discuss anything concrete but to know if they are in the office or in a place you can see them. It is preferable for all serious discussions to take place when you are with them in person. Presence is always better than phone calls when following up contacts.

TRULITOOTOO is a childcare product sales company in Victoria Island, Lagos, Nigeria. I never had the opportunity to meet the Managing Director one-on-one. However, I got her phone number from her Sales Manager. The first time I called her, she told me to meet her at 10 am the following day which was a

Saturday. I got there some few minutes to the agreed time, but she did not show up. I waited till midday before leaving. This happened repeatedly. About two 2 months after, She called to say that she had seen my samples and other materials and was very interested in them, but inability to see her in person cost me the deal. If I had seen her personally, I would not have conceded so easily. I would have pressed on with determination until the deal was signed and sealed.

From experience, I have discovered that presence is more powerful than calls. The kind of commitment your contact will put on the table when you are physically with him/her is far higher than when you are talking on phone.

You think they will call you?
I have discovered that an *"I will call you"* statement from a contact can sometimes be a dismissal. If a contact tells you that he will call you by 2.00pm tomorrow, call him when it's a few minutes past the promised time. Very few people will call especially if their call will eventually make them to sign a deal that

will make them part with some money – the benefits they would get notwithstanding. The reality that many people are finding it difficult to make ends meet has made this so. Since I started marketing, very few people actually called after they promised to call. And I have spoken to over 5000 people in the last 6 years alone. A good example is the Managing Director of MIMISTEPS, a top-notch crèche for high income earners to drop their children before going to work. I had been to her office so many times that on this particular day, she just wanted to 'get rid' of me when she got some cash.

If your contacts consistently tell you not to bother coming to see them or calling them, they are dismissing you. If they keep saying, 'I will call you when I am ready,' they have grown tired of you. Don't waste your time on them.

Persistence and consistency, the best marketing skills

Marketing theorists may not agree with me but I have discovered from first-hand experience that persistence and consistency are the best marketing skills a marketing executive requires.

Mrs. Sapphire is the Chief Executive Officer of Miss&Mr, a chain of clothing stores. I researched and got to know which of the stores she normally stays almost all day. When I first walked into the large store that occupied a whole floor in the building, she welcomed me and told me that she was interested in what I introduced to her. She only wanted to discuss with her husband first. I told her that I will be back in a few days time even though she told me that she would call me.

In a few days, I was in her shop again and she told me that she has not received any reply from her husband yet. I went there about three times the following week and got different answers but she never said she was not interested. Then, on another occasion, she said "How are we going about it?" I told her the process and procedures. Again, she somehow used another excuse to postpone her involvement. However, she did not change her mind or interest. But she was already showing signs of reluctance. Instead of letting that deter me, I engaged her in a conversation about how to make her business better. Her interest got fired up again.

Finally, on my 15th call or thereabout, she said, "Don't worry. I will call you tomorrow." At a few minutes past 10.00a.m, while I was trying to make another new contact in GRA, I got a call on my mobile phone. It was her. She asked me to come for the money at 4pm. I was elated. Some minutes past 4pm, I was at her favorite branch. But she was not in! I asked one of her sales girls about her and she said, "madam just left." While I was scolding myself and contemplating on whether to call her or wait, her white Volkswagen BORA showed through the glass door. She walked in with her usual smile. "Oga A! (Assuming A! is the name of my magazine and Oga means boss in Nigerian Pidgin) I have come." In about two minutes, she gave me the cheque and while I was writing the receipt, she said,

"Ah, what did you put in your mouth? I was not very keen on doing this deal yet, but here am I paying you!"

I will tell you what got this wonderful business woman to do business with me even though she was not too keen on doing it. It is one word and you know it. Persistence! You can say that word again. Yes persistence!

Mr. Paul has a business called MASTERPIECE. They are specialized in making hand made greeting cards. They also have some of the best works of art on sale. He is my very good friend – one that I respect so much for his words of wisdom and personality. He told me about a lady who works in the marketing department of a bank. He said that the lady wanted him to open an account with her bank. He was not interested. He said the lady came twelve times! On the twelfth time, he just had to do it.

Persistence is probably the best word in marketing. It will get you what the other marketing skills may never give to you. Writers marketing theories and formulae may not agree with me. Unless you have been on the streets before, you probably would not know what I am talking about.

If someone does not want to do business with you because he is not interested in your products or services, he will do it for another reason if you are persistent. He will do it to make you "haul your ass" off him (as John Grisham would say)!

Foolish persistence
If the prospect tells you categorically that he does NOT NEED your product or service, accept his/her decision and walk away quietly. You've got to back off. If he shows that he is interested but for some reasons, cannot make up his mind, you need persistence. But if the person starts getting irritated by your presence, it is time to let go and probably check back on the client after a long time. Otherwise, it is foolish persistence. Avoid it. A good marketer must be empathic.

Chapter 9

How to make the customer to keep buying from you

Whether you like it or not, customers will always buy. They simply can't stop buying. Your key responsibility as a marketer is to ensure that they buy from you and not from someone else. When a customer buys once, he may or may not come back. Here are a few tips you can use in sustaining their patronage. At least, if he is not buying, his friends are.

Educate your customers!
This is one important factor that will guarantee repeat patronage and increase in customers' loyalty. Education is very powerful. Your customers need to keep on learning about what makes your product or service unique and exceptional. Furthermore, teaching your customers other *ways* of using your product for maximum satisfaction can also endear you to them. For

example, there are different brands of instant noodles in Nigeria. Indomie has blossomed rapidly despite the incursion of other competing brands into the noodles market or industry. They still have the competitive advantage for several reasons. One of the reasons is that they teach people other ways of preparing Indomie noodles on TV and through other media. In one of the episodes I watched on a popular TV station, they went as far as teaching women how to prepare Indomie *Chicken Pepper Soup* for their children whenever they fall ill.

Here is another example. There are several anti-germ soaps in the market. Dettol has been having a nice time for many years because of their advertisements that are more or less like lectures. They didn't use the traditional advert concept other companies use by presenting a very pretty lady and trying to make us think that the soap made her pretty. The lady used as main character in one of their adverts is portrayed as a responsible married woman with kids. In that advert, she is seen educating viewers on the possible origin of germs and how they can make one sick. She then proffers Dettol as a reliable solution. This is education. The 'lecture' before the presentation of the product is arguably what makes many people prefer Dettol over other soaps in its category. This is not just an advertisement, but education.

Educate your customers again and again.

Prompt delivery

A customer may not pat your back if you deliver his order on time but try doing otherwise. You will risk losing him altogether if you fail to make timely amends as situation demands. An *on-time* delivery will keep a customer coming for more.

One evening, I went to visit a friend of mine, a bachelor. Since it was late, I decided to pass the night at his place. We were both hungry, but my friend had no kerosene or gas to cook. Unfortunately, the gas station had closed for the day. So, we decided to stroll to a nearby shop to get some kerosene. The owner of the shop, a lady kept us waiting for over 15 minutes (I am not exaggerating). She was engaged in a gossip with another lady who came to buy some cooking stuffs from her. There was not a single word of apology from the gossipy lady. After waiting for another 5 minutes without been attended to, we decided to keep our displeasure and anger under check by watching a match (Chelsea FC was playing Everton). My friend was very bitter. He told me that he will try as much as he can to stop going to her shop. I quickly noticed that she was the only one operating that kind of shop in that neighborhood. It dawned on me that her customers will desert her the moment they get a better option. Don't keep your customers waiting. They keep you in business!

Suggest a delivery schedule

I learnt this as a youngster. As a child, I helped my step-mum to hawk various food items on the streets of Benin City after school every day. I hawked garri (locally processed cassava flakes), yam, plantain and even kerosene. (I didn't see it as child labour/abuse and still don't! The experience has helped and is still helping me today! However, that does not mean that I am in support of child labour). Whenever someone bought from me, I instinctively asked the person to know when next I was to bring what for him. Consequently, most of my "first-time" buyers became my customers. My numerous customers made my sales activities easier and more profitable. I made tremendous sales moving from house to house with my wares. I was through before you could say "Jack Robinson". I still do it in my business today. My teams also do. This is one of the most effective ways to get a customer to keep knocking on your door!

Bonanza/Discount

A bonanza/discount can do more than attract clients to you. It can also make your customers stick to you. Whenever a bonanza is offered at special periods, I get many new clients. When the special periods are over for me to revert to the price initially considered to be very high by some, I, in end the, retain a large percentage of those new clients rather than lose them. Note that if you intend to increase the 'entry price' of a customer, it must be done in little percentages per time till it matches your expectation. Drastically increasing prices can make you lose your customers.

Options

Create options for your customers as much as you can. If you operate a company that sells products, have an inexpensive option (not the fake!) of some products for customers that cannot afford the expensive one. This is just one example of providing options for your customers.

As previously said, Indomie is one of the first noodle brands that was produced and sold in Nigeria. In my opinion, they taught Nigerians how to eat noodles. Soon, there were other noodles in the market. They (Indomie) decided to come out with different options. They have the onion flavour, chicken flavour and so on. They are still very successful in spite of the competition. This is another good example of options.

Shortly after I started my magazine business, I discovered that many businesspeople preferred television and radio adverts to magazine ads. So, I decided to go into jingles production. So, when my marketing executives and I go out and someone says "Sorry I won't be doing business with you because I want to advertise on TV," we simply smile and ask the person "how soon do we come to produce your jingle? Would you like to get a free sign-up form now?" Apart from the fact that it gets the customer to still do business with us, he does not have to use precious time looking for a studio to do his jingles. Surprisingly, many of them still end up doing the magazine advert!

Quality

My step mum never bought just anything. She always took out time to buy quality commodities for sale. One of the items she sold was garri (processed cassava flour). We always had in stock, garri for "drinking" (soaked in water with sugar or salt) and for preparing eba. Sometimes, we had a particular type that was exceptionally good at meeting both needs. So it was not difficult for me to "make customers" every time I went out to hawk. You must go out of your way to get quality. People will always crave, wait and pay for quality.

Availability

Your product or service should always be available. Can your customers still get your products during scarcity? The very first thing I ever sold *commercially* was kerosene.

Those times there were periods of kerosene scarcity all over the country, my step-mum always had to sell. She always had information of who is bringing kerosene into our city. My young hand 'touched' so much money that period. There was never a time a customer wanted kerosene and didn't get from us.

Availability is key if you want your customers to continue buying from you.

Develop a relationship
All things being equal, your friends would always buy from you. This is why you have to develop relationship with customers. Greet them like friends. The holy book says that a "friend ought to show himself friendly". You could invite one for dinner and give another a lift. You can ask yet another why he is gloomy and genuinely offer to help or advice. Offer a compliment here and there. A compliment as simple as "That dress looks nice on you" can open the door to a lasting and rewarding relationship.

Do the extra

Mr. Bayo needs a pack of writing pads. He visits 3 shops. All of them do not have it in stock. But he gets 4 different responses.

XYZ Essentials: We don't have that now, check next time.

Market Options: We don't sell such things here.

Shoppers Delight: Oh, sorry we don't have writing pads now. But I know where you can get some. Ehm...where is it again? Yes, please check Whitney Bookshop. Thanks for calling.

Super Mall: Oh, sorry we don't have writing pads now. But I know where you can get some. Can you please sit here while I go and get you some from a nearby shop?

If you were Bayo, which of the above shops would you go back to shop? A little extra will make all the difference in making a customer to keep patronizing you.

Appreciate them

You can satisfactorily appreciate a customer with just a dime. A simple thank you can go a long way in endearing yourself to the heart of that customer. Have you ever stopped a customer and say "I am very glad that you buy from us, thank you" to him in an as-a-matter-of-fact manner? It pays. I received the following text message from a fashion designer on January 2008: "A business is as good as its customer. Your patronage in 2007 is highly appreciated. We hope you will stick with us in 2008. Happy well-dressed year." If you receive that kind of text message from an organization you like patronizing, how would you feel?

Let me show you one more example. There is a pay phone centre around my house. I always go there to recharge my phone and make calls. In December 2007, I went there again. As usual, the place was full. When I finished loading the prepaid credit onto my phone, the guy who ran the place came close to me and said 'Thank you for patronizing us throughout this year." Then he handed me a steel cup. I was thrilled. I thanked him and left. When I got to my place, I looked at the cup. It was nothing – it can't be more than $1. Why was I thrilled? It was the gesture. I cannot remember where I kept that cup or what became of it as I write now. Since then, I find it difficult to enter the next shop because I don't want to be caught!

A little appreciation can get a customer committed to you.

Employ the Right People

If you want people to keep buying from you, you have to be very careful about who you employ, especially if they are going to make direct contact with clients. PREGNANT CHIC is a shop that sells clothes that are specially designed for pregnant women. These include trousers, gowns, T-shirts, just name it. I parked my car around the shop earlier on to inspect a property under renovation. As I walked back to the car, I couldn't help but notice an SUV trying to park in front of the shop. The sales girl was just locking up when the woman finished parking. The lady called to the sales girls to hold on and rushed out of her car.

Then something very disheartening happened. The sales girl turned to this lovely looking pregnant woman and said the coldest "we have closed" I have ever heard in my life. The eager, rushing customer was very disappointed. She had driven there from a place that was obviously far away. I watched to see if the sales girl would open up and help her. She just walked away towards the bus stop, leaving the woman behind.

I asked the person with me "if that were your shop, would you reopen and help this woman?" I got an emphatic "yes." I have a feeling that the sales girl would have reopened to serve the customer if the business belonged to her.

Employing the right people (people who are passionate, apt to help customers and are willing to do the extra) would result in happy customers. Happy customers make business worthwhile.

Keep Your Staff Motivated

Keep your staff motivated. A motivated work force will make happy customers. There are suggestions on how you can keep your staff motivated in this book.

Comfortable Sales Point
The sales point is either your shop, office, reception/waiting lounge. Many small companies in Lagos have really taken this to another level. You should do the same if you have not.

If you are a small-scale businessperson, I do not expect you to spend a great percentage of your capital on this, especially if you do not have adequate capital. But ensure that your business point is clean, well ventilated and disinfected to avoid flies and other insects. An air conditioner (even a fairly used one) won't be a bad idea. Nice chairs, nice floor tiles (or rug), beautiful window blinds, nicely painted walls and a few other props would provide the ambience you need to create for your customers. All these can be acquired at very reasonable prices (good thing is that you can get them all at the "fairly used market" if you cannot afford the brand new ones).

If you are operating a restaurant, people should not be eating with one hand and driving flies with the other (I have been to that kind of restaurant before! I never went back!).

Chapter 10

Marketing and your mind

There is virtually nothing you will do in life without the involvement of your mind. The mind is the greatest asset everyone is naturally endowed with. It is the site on which all the wonders of the world are first built before they are finally transferred to their physical permanent sites. The most successful people in the world are those who have understood the power of their mind and taken advantage of it. If you are going to be successful in marketing, your mind has a major role to play. It cannot play that role without your permission and cooperation.

The power of the mind

Henry Ford said that "if you think you can or think you can't, you are right." The mind is so powerful that it controls every area of your life. The aim of this chapter is to help you to understand the power of your mind. When you come to terms with how powerful your mind is, you can then take advantage of it and make a success out of your marketing job. Whether you are in the marketing department of a bank or in the sales department of a manufacturing company, the principles are the same and will work for anyone who dares to use them.

Your brain

Statistics have shown that the human brain has 20 billion cells, each of which is connected to as many as 20, 000 other cells. It is also said that what you have accomplished in life since you were a child is only a small fraction of what you are actually capable of achieving. You are not some accident in your company. You are a complex creature. Your mind is powerful! Your success starts from there. Let's roll!

Consent

One of the greatest powers of the mind is CONSENT. Have you observed that you do not actually start 'feeling' a pain until you 'consent' to it in your mind? For example, when a female friend of mine was attacked by a thief one evening, the thief mistakenly cut her hand with a knife while she was dragging her bag with him. He actually wanted to cut the bag's handle to enable fast snatching, but she was stubborn. She did not feel any pain until she got to her hostel and saw blood on her clothes. When she checked her body, she saw a cut. The moment she noticed the cut, she began to feel the pain. This is the point I call the 'moment of consent.'

Have you observed that you do not feel like peeing in your pants until you start *acknowledging* and *saying* how hard you are pressed and how much you cannot bear it? Why do people die of the diseases they are aware of faster than those they are not aware of? It is very simple. The mind. It is the power of consent! Why is it that HIV/AIDS campaigns are now focused on

146

helping its victims "stay positive" in their attitudes – in their minds?

If your mind is so powerful that it determines the outcome of the effects of the activities of your body, then it can do the same to your job or business. There is power in consent. What are you consenting to in your mind where your marketing career is concerned?

Do you fear marketing?
Over the last few years, I have developed and facilitated Effective Sales & Marketing Workshops for staff of many organizations. I always start by showing them a slide with the picture of a terrified person. The question above (DO YOU FEAR MARKETING?) seems to be jumping out of the projector screen by the side of the picture. Over 80% of the participants always say they do, including Marketing Managers and Directors! At the end of the workshop, they do not just go back to their jobs with tips, ideas and principles; but they also go back emboldened and it shows in their results! You should NEVER be scared of marketing – it is an integral part of life.

The "I can do" mentality

The power of consent is what works in the "I can do" mentality. The truth is that man cannot *really* be limited. Man can do virtually anything. Man has conquered and defied the laws of nature. We have tamed every animal, from the brave lion to the tallest giraffe to the fastest running cheetah, to the highflying eagle. We have subdued the force of gravity. Man (that includes you!) is king. Someone said that man can achieve anything he nurtures to the point of obsession in his mind. The limitations of a man are those he has consented to in his mind. The extent to which an individual can achieve anything is tied to the extent to which he has brought down the mental limitations he has erected (by him or someone else) in his mind.

Let the "I can do" mentality be your default setting whenever you are going out for marketing.

Talk your way up

Your words can make or break you. Learn to talk yourself up. Brian Tracy is one of the world's most sought after consultants who rose from being a high school dropout to becoming a global star. Brian Tracy says "begin each day by saying, 'I believe something wonderful is going to happen to me today!' And it will." He continues; "keep yourself positive by saying, 'I believe in the perfect outcome of every situation in my life.'… Control your inner dialogue. Talk to yourself *positively* all the time." The power of positive talk cannot be overemphasized. Even in marketing!

You can inspire positive self-talk by posting something positive on your wall or notice board. Write something that will make you feel on top of the world. When I begun my quest for a life of success, I heard Rev. Chris Oyakhilome say: *"I believe in the ABUNDANT life, HAPPY life and in the SUCCESSFUL life. I live in the JOYOUSEXPECTANCY of the very BEST."* Since I believed the same thing, I wrote it and placed it where I could easily see it. I signed it and wrote the following under my name: writer, publisher, speaker, entrepreneur, personal development coach. I get inspired by the things I put on the walls of my study. I love what Mike Murdoch said when he came to speak in a conference in Lagos, Nigeria. He advised that we should put pictures of our future around our houses. In other words, place photographs that depict the possible successful life that can result from being successful as a marketer, around you. Would it result in a promotion that would enable you to afford a nice car? Place photographs of the car around your house.

These pictures would inspire you to say the right words.

Determine how you want your day to be
You can determine the way the day will be while you are still in your house or office. Having made a list of the contacts you want to see on a particular day, reflect on *how* you want the day to be. You may need to say the things you expect to happen under your breath. This is called mind *conditioning*. When your mind gets inundated with this, your experience on that day will not be very different from your reflection. My friend Paul, a pastor, teacher and businessman told me that he does this whenever he is going out to negotiate a deal. He tells himself what the outcome will be and gets exactly what he has predetermined in his mind. It has

worked for me too. Have you observed that more often than not, the people you believe are nasty behave that way to you and those you believe to be nice do the same? Your absolute belief in the power behind determining the day before stepping out will produce overwhelming results as you practice it more often. It gives you an unshakable confidence that enables you to say the right things that would help you to make the sale. Trying this once and not getting expected results does not mean that it does not work. Determine the response you will get from your client before meeting him. It works.

I have a recent example. Mr. David is the Managing Director of Island Calabar Restaurant, a purely African restaurant where some of the most exotic native Calabar cuisine is on its menu. It was easy for them to do business with me. So my team and I immediately started working based on their specifications. He was never around except on some weekends. And he is in the habit of doing certain things by himself – no one else could make decisions on certain matters on his behalf. On this particular weekend, I got a tip from one of his staff that he was around. I told myself 'I am going to collect the money today, whether in cash or in cheque.' When I got there, he told me that they were considering relocating the HQ (the main outlet) of the business because of the power problems they were having as a result of the nonchalant attitude of the caretaker of the complex they were using. Therefore, he said, it would eventually be a waste for them to advertise with that address.

Normally, this should be an easy knockout for me. If someone tells me that he is relocating, I just leave the person alone. Surprisingly, I didn't let the matter rest like that. 'We have done the advert already' I told him. He was not ready to give up either. He told me that there was nothing he could do about that. After talking and talking, I threw a very good missile at him. I said "why not let us run it; when you relocate, I will mention that you people have relocated; you do not have to pay for that then." This was a GOAL!!! He told me he would accept what I just said if I agreed to collect a post-dated cheque. I accepted it and on the date that was on the cheque, what did I do with it? You can guess!

What made it possible for me not to give-up so easily? Simple! I determined that I MUST come back with cash or cheque. And didn't I?!!!

Learn to forget the bad on a good day!
Every day is good. All you need to do is focus on the good each day offers. Sometimes, a day can be very challenging if you are always on the streets. Most people end the day in a bad mood because of the challenges they faced. The way you end a day is very important. It can affect your enthusiasm and performance the following day. Do not keep your mind on the insults someone was bold enough to have unleashed on you. Rather, let your mind dwell on the nice compliments someone gave to you today. Instead of keeping your mind on the fact that some contacts told you that they are not interested in your proposal, remind yourself of those that said 'yes.' Remind yourself of those that gave you appointments.

I have never returned from street work in a bad mood. I know that sometimes, I come back almost discouraged but I don't allow the challenges of the day to make me forget the blessings that came with it. Even if no sales were made, I make myself feel good about the fact that, for example, more people are now aware of my business because whether they say yes or no, I always leave a business card, and some promotional materials. You never can tell who would see those and be interested in the nearest future!

Celebrate!
The power of celebration cannot be overemphasized. Celebrate the conquests of the day, regardless of how small you may perceive them to be. Milton Katselas was an American film director and famous Hollywood coach for The Beverly Hills Playhouse. He said that, "your career is not one big trek. It's a series of small, deliberate steps, punctuated by small celebrations. Later, as the victories become bigger, so do the celebrations." Celebrating at the end of every day helps you **to forget the bad on a good day.** Every day is

good, as I have noted before. Just look around for the blessings it offers and celebrate them! Count your blessings. Name them one by one.

What do you believe?

Your belief is very important. What you believe determines what happens around you. Someone said that your life today is a reflection of what you said yesterday. Your words are a product of your belief. Do you believe marketing is not for you? Do you believe that your skin colour will get in the way of your marketing? Do you believe that you are not good at anything? Do you believe that you will amount to nothing in life? You have to change your belief if you want to be successful in marketing or in any career in life. You can self-talk yourself out of the wrong beliefs. Your close friends and maybe your family may have told you that you can only be average in the things you do in life. But the truth is that you can do above average. You can be exceptional. My pastor, Dr. Isaiah Wealth taught me how to self talkmyself to believe what will take me higher in life. He said "you have to tell yourself 'I believe I will be successful, I don't believe I will fail. I believe in a life of abundance. I don't believe in lack.'" Jim Donovan further explains this concept in his book, Take Charge of your Destiny: "…The problem is, most of us have a *limiting belief* in our ability to accomplish a particular task. We only tap into a small portion of our potential, take limited action and produce a poor result….if you develop a belief you can do whatever you set your mind to, you will tap into more of your limitless potential, take massive amounts of action, and produce even greater results."

Make it habitual

Your habits, they say, can either make or break you. And that is true, you know. You have to make the project of *believing the best of you* to become a habit. I strongly agree with what Aileen Ludington and Hans Diehl said in their book, Health Power, Health by Choice Not Chance, a book I recommend for everybody young and old. They said this about habits "True, they (habits) can oil the machinery of our lives, helping us glide through our days, saving time and energy. (Who would want to have to stop and think how to tie a pair of shoelaces, after all?) But habits can make our lives more difficult as well – and if you doubt that, try changing sides of the bed with your spouse tonight!"

So, how will you make yourself habitually develop an "I can do" mentality? Aileen and Hans explained so much about habit formation in their book. But let me not bore you with technical terms. They said it takes about 3 weeks to form one new habit. They gave this example: "A few years ago, for instance, a woman named Anya Bateman decided to start flossing her teeth. What had been a tiresome chore, she learned, evolved into a bedtime ritual in less than a month. Encouraged, she applied her 3 week plan to breaking her habit of eating too many sweets. Next she broke her habit of criticizing her husband, then formed a new habit of praising her kids. The results were so astounding that they were published in Reader's Digest."

In the next 3 weeks, why not wake up in the morning and start *conditioning* your mind. Soon, it will become a habit and you will start producing the results of a champion!

Mind conditioning
The mind can be conditioned just the way a room can be air-conditioned. You can condition your mind to begin to think in a *certain way*. Mind conditioning is very important in building beliefs. We have already discussed how your beliefs can affect your performance on the job. What are those things you have been told by friends, family, circumstances and society that you cannot do? Simply write them down and take an objective look at them. Can you do them? Can you become good at them if you *really want to*? Take out about 10 minutes daily to *affirm* that you can do those things. Remember what we said before about consent. The affirmation here helps to build your *consent* in the positive. In Philemon 1:6, the Apostle Paul said that "the communication of your faith (or your way of life) is made effectual by the *acknowledging* of every good thing that is in you." Acknowledging every good thing in you (your potential, talents and abilities) helps you to condition your mind to give you the right feedback that

is required to make you the success you want to be in life.

Mind Tonics

Maybe you have not heard of this before but there are mind tonics. These are virtues and activities that help to give you the right mind-set. Do you want your mind to be well "tuned" to give you the right feedback you need for a successful career? Use mind tonics! Mind tonics are as follows:

- Joy: Always maintain a joyful attitude.
- Contentment: Contentment keeps you from jealousy, envy and strife. Appreciate what you have.
- Forgiveness: This is another very important tonic to your mind. Have you noticed that there is always a feeling of a weight being lifted from your shoulder whenever you forgive someone for real?
- Originality: Be yourself. Work on self improvement and be your best.

- Reading the right stuff: You know what is right for you. You don't always have to read materials that do not inspire you to be and do better. Do you?

- Celebrate and appreciate others: Learn to see the good in other people. Avoid destructive criticisms. Speak nicely to people.

There's more but the Apostle Paul summarizes it as 'whatsoever things are true, whatsoever things *are* honest, whatsoever things *are* just, whatsoever things *are* pure, whatsoever things *are* lovely, whatsoever things *are* of good report; if *there be* any virtue, and if *there be* any praise, think on these things.' (From Acts 4: 8, KJV)

Mind Poisons

Poisons of the mind are the direct opposite of mind tonics. They are hatred, bitterness, envy, alcohol, tobacco and many, many more. You were employed in your company to be efficient. Your mind is the most important asset the company wants from you. If not, they would have employed anyone other than you. Don't destroy your mind.

Yes you can! Will versus Ability

Did I hear you say you can't? Why? I had reasons to say I can't when I wanted to start my publishing company. But I did not. I studied Science Laboratory Technology in the university and had no training in journalism. But I have always wanted to help people. I have always wanted to write things that will inspire them to stand their ground and make a groundbreaking reality out of their dreams. Magazine publishing was the means I wanted to use to steer this desire. After writing a business plan and designing a concept for the magazine, I went to see my friend and business mentor at the time, Honorable NosaIzore, a notable Rotarian. When I showed him my plans, he gave me words of encouragement alongside some well-needed "fatherly" advice.

A few months later, I was in his office again, this time with the first edition of my brainchild A!, a 56 paged full colour glossy pages magazine. He was elated when I handed him a copy. He paid me for the copy immediately and tore off the transparent packaging material, began to go through it, page by page with the kind of seriousness I have always known him for, while I looked on. When he finished, he took a deep breath and said this looking into my eyes: "Kingsley, I admire your doggedness. Do you know that I have always wanted to publish a magazine since I was young? But here you are with no training in journalism. You have published one. If you continue this way, the sky only will be your limit." Hon. Izore studied Mass Communication in the United States and therefore had the training and hence the ability to make his magazine publishing dream a reality. He also had the financial resources to do it but he didn't.

What did he intend to make me learn from this? It's profound – strong will is better than ability. There are many people who have ability but lack enough strong will. You probably do not have a formal training in marketing - but that is not a problem. Personally, I do not have any formal training in marketing except for some studies I have done on my own, but I have tangible results in the field of marketing. Wait a minute.

I can hear your boss saying that the results count more than the training. The reason for the training is the results. Go for all the training you need. However, a strong will can produce tremendous results in the absence of training. Develop your will. The will would help you get 'on-the-job' trained, by all means possible.

A sound heart is the life of the flesh (body): but envy the rottenness of the bones (Proverbs 14:30)

Chapter 11

You are a Marketer!

Day-to-day living is all about marketing. There is a marketer in everyone. You are a marketer. The better marketer you are, the more friends you make and keep. Whether you know it or not, there are certain people who admire and look up to you. They see in you what you personally may not consider a big deal. People's perception of you is what generally motivates them to want to identify with you or with what you do. This perception is created by the words you speak, the clothes you put on, the way you treat others, the way you listen, the way you smile and many other interpersonal skills you may have. There are certain people who may not even make very important decisions until they have consulted you. There are those who like to confide in you whenever they are in a situation. The measure to which people look up to an individual differs from the measure to which they look up to another; it all depends on their perception of each person. The reason for all this analysis is to help you understand that you are responsible for the way people relate with you. No matter what your experience with people may be, the marketer in you has been expressing himself/herself in various ways. Even if it is only one person in the whole world that responds favourably to you, it is the marketer in you that made it to happen.

All you need do is to acknowledge this and begin to develop the marketer in you to become better. Before we go into all that, I want us to explore some of the things the marketer in you has achieved or done before.

What The Marketer In You Has Done Before

Interaction

Human life is entwined in constant communication. It is the marketer in you that helps you to interact with people to a point where they like you and probably become your close acquaintances. You interact with your friends, family, lecturers, co-workers, staff, boss and many other people around you. The marketer in you makes it possible to communicate with these people and have them to value their relationship with you.

Wrote your exams

Writing examinations is a persuasive exercise. That you wrote and passed at least one examination shows that you are a marketer. You read your notes and in your own words, gave them back to your teachers or lecturers. It took the marketer in you to present those facts to them and get them to agree with you and give you the grades you deserved.

Got you a spouse

If you are a man and are the one that went after your spouse (some ladies do initiate relationships and propose marriage these days!), you are a good marketer. You succeeded in selling what you perceived of your future to a woman and she agreed to be a part of it as your wife. You made her to dare to fall in love with you just by speaking those words and by exuding those characteristics that made her to say 'hmmm. I like this guy.' You are a great marketer!

If you are a lady and you are married or have a man in your life, you are a great marketer, probably a greater one than the man. You were most likely on your own and that guy came over to ask you out and things started happening from there. What did he see? Whatever the qualities are, you were able to market them by wearing the right clothes, smiling the right way, talking in a peculiar way and so on. You are a great marketer

Got you a job
Do you have a job in any firm or are you in business? If you are an employee, the marketer in you got you the

job. You were able to convince the employer, beyond all reasonable doubts, that you were the right candidate for the job. You did it by writing a most impressive application letter and a nice CV, and proving yourself to be the best for the job during the interview. This is the marketer in you.

Got you membership into a club
Are you a member of any exclusive club in your town? What got you membership into it and keeps you there is the marketer in you.

Got you a position in your organization
Did you contest for and win a seat in the executive council of an organization you belong to? The marketer in you helped you. Even if you didn't win, the marketer in you got you the votes you got!

Got you invitation to that party
People invite only those they like and consider important to their parties and memorable events. The fact that you were invited shows that you are, at least, somewhat a good marketer

How To Develop The Marketer In You

Some people think that they are never good at anything. If you are in those shoes, you need to change your perception of you. It is important to do this especially if you are interested in making it in marketing and in business. Learn with close friends and acquaintances. Be natural because some people would easily know when you are being artificial. Anyone can do the following to develop the natural marketer in them.

Smile at people

Smiling is very powerful and can be contagious. Learn to smile at people. It can make someone's day and help to develop the marketer in you. Customers are more comfortable to listen to a smiling marketer than to a straight-faced one. You can develop yourself to be a habitual "smiler."

Be polite to people

Learn to politely say an enthusiastic "Hello!" to people. That simple gesture activates the polite person in you. It is very important in developing the marketer in you.

Learn to listen

In developing the marketer in you, you need to be a good listener. Customers like to do business with good listeners. And when you listen, listen attentively and show it. Encourage the person with 'yeah,' a nod, and so on.

Give, give and give

What do you have to give? Give to people. Render assistance to someone. Give them your time, give them money, and give them of your knowledge. Be apt to give. Be a helper. Gestures of giving can make you develop into a better marketer as you will begin to naturally see yourself trying to help a customer. Your sales will obviously not look like a selfish one because you will be more interested in helping the customer to get the best from doing business with you. And customers prefer to do business with those they perceive to be helping them.

Read

Read books that deal with how to get along with people and get them to like you.

Keeping in touch

Always keep in touch with your friends no matter how far away they are. Keeping in touch with your family, friends, schoolmates can help develop your ability to make people like and value you. It is highly needed in marketing.

Dress well

Dress the way you want to be perceived by people. Dress like a knowledgeable and powerful person. Don't put anything on because it is in vogue. Be modest in your dressing. If you are not satisfied by what you see in your mirror after dressing up, change into something better.

Show people that you respect them

People get turned on to like you if you respect them and show that you do. I have learnt this so much that I can call a youngster "madam" or "sir." People love to be treated with respect. Even if you resent someone, you have to kill that feeling and show some respect. It is difficult but when you perfect it, it will help you on the streets when you are doing business with people. There are people who are going to treat you badly when you meet them to do business with you. If you get emotional and take it personal, you have lost a prospect and all the prospects he would have referred to you. Now that does not mean you should take "bullshit" from everyone. Just always remember that if you need to close any door, it is wise to do it quietly and peacefully as you may need that door again soon.

Chapter 12

Avenues for marketing

Getting opportunities to carry out marketing activities is not difficult for big companies because marketing is an integral part of their budget. It is not always so for small and medium scale business entrepreneurs who may not have adequate funds at their disposal. I have suggested some ideas below. You can use as many of them as possible to promote your business. Use those that suit the business environment of your country.

Seminars/Workshops: Watch out for dates and venues of seminars and workshops in the city where you do business. Then contact the organizers before the day and ask for a few minutes to talk to the participants and distribute your marketing materials. You may want to give a special offer to the first 5 or 10 people who have agreed to do business with you. You can even get people to work for you for a commission from this kind of gathering, depending on the age group. If you have a few thousands to spare, you can be a part-sponsor of such events.

Cooperatives: You may contact the various cooperatives in the city or town your business is located and make them do business with you at a commission. Since they are often interested in assisting their members to acquire certain products for their business or personal use; cooperatives would be a good bet if you deal with such products. They can also allow you to introduce your offer(s) to their members.

Market Women Association: This is almost the same as cooperatives above. The main difference is that these associations may sometimes not be for hard-core business purpose like cooperatives. It could just be for "social" reasons. If you are a dealer in consumer products, this is a very good avenue to sell and to generate references.

Places of worship: This could be very difficult depending on the kind of leaders in charge. Some may want you to speak with their members if what you have to offer is very important. You may want to place your materials in their reception areas, information desks, or if they agree on seats or pews.

A very easy way out is to understand the structures they have in place and gradually market your way through them. Some operate in little groups such as youths, singles, married, about-to-marry classes, mothers and fathers' groups.

Buses/trains: This avenue is very popular in Nigeria and in Africa. Some people travel in a bus for the sole purpose of advertising and selling their products to the passengers. You do not have to do this. You may send your sales people to the bus or train stations to talk to people before they travel. If it is not a product that can easily be moved around (or if it is a service), use beautiful fliers, fact sheets, etc for this.

Fast food centres: Fast food restaurants spring up everywhere everyday. Many of them have loyal customers. Hence this is one of the fastest ways to get people to know about your business. This is the major avenue I used when I was pursuing adverts for the magazine I published in 2007. I placed copies in almost every fast-food restaurant in my City. I wrote "Don't take away please" on the front of each copy. The result was that almost everyone we contacted to do business with us agreed to because the magazine was 'everywhere.' Distribution of your marketing materials can be sweat-free and effectively done through these restaurants. All you need to do is place them on the counter where people can easily pick them up.

Supermarkets: There are many supermarkets across Nigeria (some of which I have never been to) where some of my products are sold. If your product or service does not pose a threat to their business, you can contact the local supermarket managers for permission to use their supermarket as an outlet. You just have to be prepared to pay them a commission.

Airports: Depending on what you have for sale, the local airport is a great place to market products or services.

Petrol stations: This one is easy. If you are able to win the manager of a petrol station to your side, he may ask his sales people to hand your marketing materials to people as they attend to them.

Bookshops: This is another good avenue for carrying out marketing for your business. The manager may agree that you insert your marketing materials in his books. Whoever buys gets the materials.

Cyber cafés: You can place a marketing material in front of each PC in a public cyber café. Alternatively, you may want to hand them over to the cashier that sells tickets to their customers. Then he hands the materials alongside the ticket. Simple, isn't?

Walls, trees, etc: This depends on where you live. Fliers are not allowed in my city.

Campuses: If your target customers are students or their age range, you need to look elsewhere. The students centre, hostel common rooms, shopping malls and restaurants are the best places to consider.

The internet: The internet has become one of the best means of carrying out marketing activities. You can design and launch a website that suits your needs.

However, you have to ensure that you get an expert to do it for you. There's more on this in the last chapter of this book.

IMPORTANT

You will need to use these methods based on who your target customers are, where they can be found and the best way to reach them. What works for business 'A' may not work for business 'B'.

Chapter 13

Is Marketing Theory Important?

"Go beyond theory. Learn down to earth easy-to-understand practical principles on getting and keeping clients."

The quote above is found on the back cover of this book. Before the final stages of editing the book, the following words were also on the back page – "whenwe get to the field (streets), our experience is often different from what we read in the 'marketing books' and learnt in 'marketing seminars.' Then it dawns on us that it was all mere theory…"

Obsolete Ideas

Do these statements mean that theory (what the experts are saying) is not important? Well, theory is very important. The only challenge we have with theory is that some of them are based on other theories, probably older ones. And things are changing with time. The theories that worked in the 1930s may not work right now. Have you ever wondered why some textbooks on entrepreneurship are very boring and why students complain about the course in some universities? It is simple – the lecturers who write such textbooks base them on other texts that were written decades ago. Moreover, most of them have never run a profit-oriented business before. You cannot teach what you have not tested.

Education

Another reason the theory in marketing does not help many businesspeople is that many of them are not educated. For example, the Ibos from eastern Nigeria are known to be very enterprising. They are so enterprising that can find them in every city and town in the country doing business. Many of them start business apprenticeship with their uncles, aunts etc. immediately after their secondary school. Some of them do not even go to secondary school before learning some trade. But many of them end up owning large businesses. If they do not go back to school, a "marketing book" may be too technical for them. But that does not mean that technical marketing texts are not important.

So, you should not avoid reading "marketing theory" books if you can understand them. They are important.

Many of the experts may not have started and run a business before but they make a lot of sense and can help you to a large extent. Lecturers of various disciplines – botany, microbiology, biochemistry, etc. – teach a medical student before he finally becomes a doctor. They may not be medical doctors, but they will end up making a good doctor out of that student.

WHY THEORY IS IMPORTANT

It helps you to know what to expect

If you have never gone out to carry out marketing activities for your company before, reading a marketing text helps you to know what to expect. It may not be presented in such a way that you will be able to adapt it to your own situation or business, but you can measure if the methods you are about to use are okay.

It helps you to make the necessary preparations

Reading technical marketing texts can help you to make the necessary preparations that you need to make a success out of your marketing initiatives. Whether you are able to grasp the analysis or not, you will be able to prepare based on certain vital information in the text.

It brings confidence

Confidence is everything in sales and marketing. Information boosts confidence. Therefore, your duty to yourself and to your business is to ensure that you keep getting information no matter how technical or difficult it may seem. It will definitely make you more confident while in the field.

It helps you to get the job

If you are a job seeker, you never can tell who is going to interview you for that marketing job. It is therefore important to learn the technical part of the subject. The interviewer may choose to make the interview very technical and theoretical.

It helps you to learn more

Someone said that the more you learn, the more you can learn. These texts, no matter how technical they are will definitely expand your mind. They will help you to be able to see and judge things from the right point of view.

It saves time

The time spent on trying to experiment on the methods to employ in your marketing quest can be saved if you are able to stumble across a little note, idea, example etc in a marketing text.

There are many more reasons. Texts on marketing theory are good. If you can, try as much as possible to read and understand them. But it is (if not more) important to read books that are written by people who have been on the field. Practical experience is important. That is why you always insist on employing people with experience.

Chapter 14

Marketing & Systems

So far, much has been said about marketing in this book. I believe that anyone can be good at marketing if they adopt the suggestions in this book, and in other books that have dealt extensively with the subject. Having an effective marketing management process is the key to attracting and retaining customers and hence, business growth. But not everyone can effectively *manage* this process irrespective of how good they are at marketing. Management is all about being able to set up and run systems to ensure maximum productivity. It is therefore imperative for you to have systems in place that can effectively run the marketing process, no matter how small your business may be. This is what makes you a manager.

What are systems?

A system is a structure that ensures that a business runs perfectly irrespective of the owner or manager. It involves formulation and deployment of certain parameters that your people (or workers) can depend on to ensure utmost efficiency. A system offers you the opportunity to manage the people that manage your business, instead of running your business directly. Have you ever heard about "Standard Operating Procedures?" That is an example of what systems are.

WHY YOU NEED SYSTEMS IN MARKETING

Limited results: If you want to go beyond just making a few sales in order to keep your business running, you have to put systems in place. Having an efficient system would enable you to make as many sales as you desire without too much effort.

Results vs. Activities: Systems help your workers to be able to practically differentiate between activities from results, and pursue more results.

Manage people; let them manage the business: Systems help you to manage people instead of trying to directly manage every aspect of your business. The people in turn would manage your business.

Have some fun! Have more profits: Having a system in place will help you to have more time for yourself. They avail you of the opportunity to make more profits because your staff will become more productive and also give you enough time to have fun.

Growth: Generally, having a system in place is what triggers growth in many organizations. Let's take the Nigerian banking sector as an example. Each bank has several branches nationwide. All the branches do almost the same thing. Staff in one branch dress the way staff in other branches dress. Many of the banks have the same pattern of buildings everywhere. They achieve all these and more through systems. No bank Managing Director is trying to visit all the branches of his bank. There are systems that ensure that things work and grow accordingly.

Systems keep your business activities simple: Just imagine you were the Managing Director of a bank. How will you visit all the branches in 365 days? It becomes easier to run the business when you employ the use of systems. If you are interested in growing that business or increasing its market share, you have to employ systems.

THE SYSTEMS YOU NEED IN MARKETING
Records

Keeping records is vital to the growth of every business. Therefore, you should have a system in place that gathers and keeps records for present and future use. For example, if your workers are writing and submitting reports, say, every weekend, there should be a system that collates them. Also, there should be a system that keeps and updates a database of your clients/customers.

Customer calls

There should be a system that ensures that customers are called when required. How often should a staff call a customer? Instead of you taking on the responsibility of telling each of your marketing staff what to do, the system shows them what to do. For example, you could put an operating procedure in place that ensures that enquiries are attended to within one hour. Another procedure could be that customers are called every one week until they make a purchase. Such systems make things work with or without your direct supervision.

Targets

What is the target for each staff? There should be a system that ensures that they are hitting their targets. Keeping a good record system can greatly aid this. Many managers have used this to scare away rather good workers by setting unrealistic targets for them. A target should not be overwhelming. In fact, the staff's remuneration should be a logical percentage of their target.

Customer service and complaints

How do you want certain customer complaints treated? Develop a system for it. Don't just allow someone's complaints to be treated on impulse. Systems help customers to be satisfied irrespective of your marketing staff's mood. The airhostess for example, smiles at you whether she feels good or not. Systems make it possible.

Remuneration & incentives

What system do you have for paying your staff? Is salary based on a paper (certificate) or on performance? What level of performance earns what? What qualifies one for a package of incentives? Determine this and develop a system out of it. This ensures that people get to earn based on their efforts. It consequently encourages the culture of hard work.

Communication

There should be a system to ensure a free flow of information. Every major decision by management may be posted on the company's notice board, on the website, or sent through email. No matter what method is employed, it is important to have a system in place for this.

Discipline

What system is in place for remanding erring workers? You need to have such in place to avoid partiality.

Money

What happens to the money when it comes? Into which accounts do you pay the money? Some companies accept cash while others don't. They would rather you go to the bank and pay the money directly into their accounts. What system do you want to use? It is up to you to decide.

Learning

There must be a system that ensures that everyone on your marketing team is constantly learning. How often do you and your staff attend refresher courses? What is the number of books they should read per month? What measure do you have in place to check if they are actually reading?

MARKETING SYSTEMS

Every manager is paid to manage people through systems. If the systems are working well, he needs not worry about output and results. Whenever there is a problem with any system, all he needs do is to help the person(s) (systems are about people) in that system or adjust the parameters that run the system.

As a manager, you may not work in the field but you determine what goes on there based on the system you have developed. If there are holes in the system there will be leakage. Systems are meant to conserve energy, potential and resources and harness them to produce the desired goals of the organization. Since marketing is one the integral parts of the organization, it is important to put a marketing system in place.

A marketing system makes marketing activities to run smoothly and successfully. It is good to be a great sales or marketing person, however, being a great marketing manager is a different ball game. You cannot ensure that your people are getting clients/customers merely by telling them what to do. You do it through established systems.

When I first started going out for marketing with my staff, I could not understand why I was getting so *much more* results than them. At that point, all we sold was advertisement on my magazine. They used to tell me that I got more results because my picture was on the publisher's page. I did not believe because there were people who already agreed to do business with me before they even discovered that I was the publisher. My breakthrough came when I decided to separate the business from me.

Marketing Cycle

I just told myself that it was time to study the trend. Why would someone not agree to do business with A and agree to do with B even though they are selling the same product? So I wrote down some important points on all the times I was successful. It was almost the same thing. Then I designed what I called a marketing cycle. Do you know what a cycle is? The Oxford Advanced Learners' Dictionary defines a cycle as "a series of events that are regularly repeated in the same order." In marketing, the cycle starts at the first call on the prospect and ends at the moment where exchange (payment and delivery) occurs.

What is the marketing cycle for the product or services in your company? Have you taken out time to think about it? If not, why not do it now. Write every detail. Then, train people to work with the various phases of the cycle. Watch as they use this cycle and adjust it until it produces the results you desire. This kind of cycle can be used to design a system.

Money in the system

I once had a very effective staff in my sales department. He was so good that I had to put him in charge of a large zone. When it was time for everyone on the team to remit money, he complained that some things came up and he had to borrow the money (without my permission) to settle them. At that time, that money was very big to me. It was needed to run the business. He promised to pay back as soon as possible. It is over 4 years now and he is yet to pay back. I said that to help you understand why you need to include the handling of money in your system. Every staff should know that the handling of cash for too long can be very tempting. If you are dealing with a client that has a current account, ask for a cheque. However, if he does not have a cheque and is paying cash, the marketing personnel should take the money to the bank and pay it into the company's account. Alternatively, the customer can either pay online or be given access to a POS Device.

Non-paying strong prospect

This is what we do in my company. If a marketing staff is convinced that he has met a very strong prospect but for one reason or another, is not able to get the sale, he reports back to the office. Management then decides to send someone else back to the prospect. And the results are always wow! I devised this because of my experience with the Managing Director of N's, an event planning firm. Rita, one of my most effective marketing staff visited the firm, met the MD and told her about our offer. She said that she was not interested. When I went there myself, I did not talk much. She agreed to do business with us immediately.

New light

Let's consider this in another light. Have you ever taken time to draw the organizational structure of your business? I used to think that such 'diagrams' were merely drawn to show us the order of seniority in a company. But it is more than that. It has a lot to do with systems. Drawing one for your company and determining what happens at each level is a good step in designing a system for your company. All Microsoft products work independent of Bill gates. It is so because they sell software. Software is designed to produce results independent of the designer. Software is the system that gives a computer the ability to carry out certain functions. Learn the principle behind software and you will be able to design a good system for your company.

In designing a system for your company, separate yourself from it (whether you are going to be involved or not). Then step into your place in the system and remove yourself from it every now and then to check and make improvements.

Chapter 15

When Marketing does not Help You

Marketing is supposed to help you because it is the lifeline of your business. If your business is not responding to marketing efforts, chances are that it (the business) is not meeting needs, solving problems or not well packaged. Another reason could be that your business is deficient in other areas like delivery, consistency, or you are simply copying someone else's business without proper innovation. There could be other reasons. Let us look at some of the basic areas you need to look at if your business appears not to be responding to marketing.

Needs & Problems

Every business is meant to meet a need or solve a problem. Any enterprise that is started without the sole aim of meeting at least a need or solving a problem will not work. Even if it works initially, it will crumble. When your business does not respond to marketing, take a writing pad and a pen. Reflect again on the needs your business was meant to meet in the first place. Write them down. Then ask yourself specific questions like: do these needs exist or did I just think they do? Do people see these as problems; do they see them as needs? Finally, do the needs and problems *still* exist? If you are absolutely certain that your business is actually meeting needs or solving problems that people are *aware* of and would want them met or solved respectively, there is still hope for the business. Move on to the next point.

Methods

As a result of the rate at which the world changes today, every businessperson ought to constantly review their methods. What methods is your business adopting to meet the needs it was set up for? Are the methods becoming obsolete? What do you need to do to improve on the methods? This is very important because the reason people are not doing business with you after your marketing efforts could just be your methods. Improve on your methods and business processes. Don't forget to write exactly what it is you are going to improve in your methods. There were times when manual photography was predominant. Gradually, digital photography crept in. Soon, everyone was more interested in digital photography. The reason is not far-fetched. In manual photography, you can only see your pictures after they have been printed. However, in digital photography, you can actually see the pictures and select the ones you want printed. Moreover, they can be copied onto a CD for those who want to use them to design websites, fliers, magazines, etc. (As a magazine publisher, I am really glad that this is possible because there is a great difference between using digital photographs and scanning printed photographs. Moreover, if you are not able to get good pictures, it may be difficult to get the celebrity again for another photo session). Personally, I cannot stand posing before manual cameras. I will only do it if the photographer is really good, probably an award winner! Anyone who wants to stick with the former (old) method in photography will definitely wallow in obscurity. Marketing will not help him.

Competition
If your competition is far better or bigger than you, your marketing efforts may become fruitless. What are you supposed to do if this is the case? Look for those areas where your competitor does not reach and concentrate your marketing efforts there. Get closer to the grassroots. There are many big companies that

produce nice toilet soaps in Nigeria. When you say 'toilet soap,' names like Lux, Joy, Dettol, Delta and Imperial Leather comes to mind. But many soap-making companies are springing up everyday because of the rapid growth of industrialization and entrepreneurial quest in the country.

They are all having a nice time despite the influence of the bigger companies. These smaller companies engage sales people who move from place to place to convince people to use their products. They go to schools, bus stops and other points they can find people. Note that these companies do not have enough money to do the big advertisements (like bill boards, national TV ads, glossy magazines etc.) like the bigger companies. Yet they sell by getting closer to people. There is always a way to outwit your competitor, no matter how big he is. There is a valuable lesson in what Rupert Murdoch said. He said that, "the world is changing fast. Big will not beat small anymore. It will be the fast beating the slow." How remarkable! Get faster than your competitor.

If your competitor is better than you are, step up. Improve your methods.

Price

Is everyone saying that what you are offering is too expensive? If people think your offer is too expensive, marketing may not help. Before Globacom started operations in Nigeria, there were already two mobile telecommunications providers in operation. We were paying so much for less talk. I bought my line for over fifteen thousand naira (about $95). When Globacom came in, they sold their lines for less than one thousand naira (compare that with how much I bought mine). They also introduced per second billing which the first two said was impossible. The results were astounding. Almost all my friends migrated to the new network. Even my dad who refused to use a mobile phone because it was expensive to buy and maintain bought one immediately. Many Nigerians who may never have afforded the use of mobile phone started using. Today, even children of 10 have mobile phones. The marketing efforts of the others could not move people like my father to join their networks because they regarded them as too expensive.

What should you do if your price is too high? Review your processes. It could just be that your prices are too high because you are using expensive means to produce your products and services. There are cheaper ways of getting things done without compromising quality. Brainstorm with your team. Get on the Internet, read books, carry out research, consult experts and see what you can do to reduce production costs. Another way out could be to increase the quantity of goods produced per time. In that way, cost is distributed among more goods.

If they still complain about the price or if it is impossible to change the price, then repackage, re-brand, do anything that will change people's perception to your products or services. People's perception is what determines if they will tag something expensive or not.

Packaging

Bad packaging will affect your marketing. So, repackage! Work on your wrappers, work on your label. Make it more attractive. Most times, people actually pay for packaging and not necessarily the product. If you are running a service-providing firm, work on your marketing materials. It creates people's first impression of you. Brainstorm with your team and see how you can repackage. Call your business Consultant. Let him guide you.

Delivery

If your delivery methods are not good enough, marketing may not help you. Review the way goods and services are delivered by your firm and fill every loophole.

Systems

If customers are not responding to your marketing efforts, it could be that you have holes in your systems. Look at your systems again and re-organize. Sometimes, it could just be that your marketing is good enough but the systems to ensure that efforts and processes are utilized is either not functional or not in place at all.

Inadequate running funds

If this is your problem, seek partnership. There is power in it. But don't forget to seek expert advice before going into partnership with anybody. You would also need an Exit or Partnership Termination Plan/Strategy in place. The plan should be agreed upon by all parties involved.

Machinery Vs. Manpower

Are you using machines or manpower? This could be the reason you are having problems. I once started and ran a cleaning and laundry firm called Pristine Cleans. My marketing was superb but the finishing (the end product) was not good enough. I was using manpower instead of machinery. I used to encourage my staff to do better; that we were going to get washing, drying and other kinds of machines soon. But using machine was still the best. It saves time, conserves energy and increases the chances that the customer comes back. When the problem persisted because of my inability to get the required funds to buy the required machines, I quit the business since I did not want to go into partnership for certain reasons.

Plan

Consult your business plan again. See if you are doing what the plan says. Review it to know if what you have there is based on assumption. Check if it is your marketing plan that has a problem and work on it again.

Customer

You may want to blame your failure in making your marketing efforts worthwhile on your customers. The truth is that the customer is always right. He is right and you must give him what he wants. I have given my own example before. The first edition of my first magazine did not sell as I anticipated it would. It dawned on me that I was giving readers what I thought was best for them. As much as I love personal development, I changed the concept of the magazine leaving just a fraction to personal development. I packed it with entertainment and the customers made me smile. The customer is always right.

Looking at this in another light, you may be pursuing the *wrong* customer. Did I say the wrong customer? Yes, it is not a mistake. You cannot sell a freezer to the Eskimos, can you? They don't need it. You cannot sell a pair of ice-skates to a Nigerian who lives in Nigeria! Someone said "you can't sell dog food to dogs." Don't try to tell a dog about how good your brand is. He may like it but it's his owner that will buy from you. If you sell farming tools and accessories, the TV may not be the best medium to use for marketing. Ensure that you are pursuing the right customer with the right product or service.

Staff
If you employ the wrong people, your business is not in safe hands. What experience do your workers give to customers when they come to do business with you? There is a popular fast food centre around my office.

They spend so much money on advertisements. But their manager in this particular outlet is very nasty and ill-mannered. As much as I like to patronize them, I don't go to that particular outlet.

You need to constantly investigate to ensure that your customers are being treated right. If a staff member treats me disrespectfully, I can forgive them if they apologize. I can even ignore it if they do it unknowingly. But they know that treating a client disrespectfully is unpardonable.

You

The problem may be YOU. Maybe you have not developed enough skills that would make a business work. What should you do? Quit being a businessperson? No! Get yourself a business mentor. There are many successful businesspeople out there who would love to mentor those who are still coming up. What you are doing right now by reading this book shows that you believe in improvement. Only people who truly desire improvement read. Get more books on business and personal development. Improve on yourself. Improve on your business skills. Read biographies of people who have succeeded in their own fields. Doing this might just be your way out of frustration.

Getting Local isn't Really Bad

Entrepreneurs are always excited about going national and international even before they are able to convince their next-door neighbor to buy from them. Well, there is nothing wrong with dreaming big, but it is better to learn to crawl before learning to run. Often, when we start our marketing efforts, we want to cover the whole country overnight. The impact may not be felt this way especially if you do not have unlimited budget for marketing as the big companies do. If you have been trying to cover the whole country before your locality, you are sponsoring your own frustration. It will be necessary therefore to get successful locally and expand gradually.

Brainstorm for more reasons why you think marketing is not helping your business and make the necessary adjustments.

Chapter 16

Is your business socially responsible?

The moment you start making money from your business, it is important to start giving something back. This is when social responsibility comes in. Being socially responsible can help your business. It cannot be entirely separated from marketing because it is also people-oriented. It would also contribute to your PR. The Oxford English Dictionary defines the word "responsible" as "having the job or duty of doing something or caring for somebody/something, so that one may be blamed if something goes wrong." No wonder the experts have defined Corporate Social Responsibility as the "ethical, legal and philanthropic behaviour in the workplace, market and community."

In being socially responsible, we are told that your business is accountable for its employees, the community, and the environment. Your employees are people, there are people in the community (where your market is) and the environment affects the people. I can therefore redefine corporate social responsibility as being sensitive to, and identifying with the needs and yearnings of the people who are within the sphere of contact of your business. These people are your employees, your customers and those who reside around your business location who may not necessarily buy from you.

RESPONSIBILITY TO YOUR CUSTOMERS

Your first responsibility is to your customers. When you go out to find out for sure what your customers want (or need) and put resources, manpower and other factors together to ensure that you are able to get them what they want, you are socially responsible. The

Nigerian National Agency for Food and Drug Administration and Control (NAFDAC) under the leadership of Dr. Dora Akunyili is a good example of a socially responsible agency. During her tenure as Director General of the agency, she successfully closed down the businesses of selfish individuals who were irresponsible enough to make harmful concoctions and sell them to the public as drugs or beverages. There are many companies who have become very successful because they put their customers first.

RESPONSIBILITY TO YOUR STAFF

Your workers are the most valuable resources in your business. Your responsibility to your staff is what makes your responsibility to your customer evident. If workers are disgruntled and not happy with their employer, it will show in their services. They will scare customers away. What are your responsibilities to your staff? Your duty to the people that work with you are as follows:

1. A conducive working atmosphere free of avoidable hazards, harassment, bullying and so on;

2. Their development: constant training to keep them enthused, focused and well-informed;

3. Prompt payment of salaries and other entitlements as at when due; and

4. Recreation especially if the nature of the job demands that they work for long hours.

RESPONSIBILITY TO THE ENVIRONMENT

Your responsibility to the environment includes effective disposal of waste materials and involvement in the efforts of conservation organizations.

RESPONSIBILITY TO THE COMMUNITY

Social responsibility can actually increase patronage if you plan it very well. It can trigger loyalty. One of the most common ways in which companies activate this today is by sponsoring events. Such events could be a local dinner to honour an illustrious citizen of a community, a youth jamboree or a community-empowerment lecture. No matter what it is that you have decided to sponsor, just ensure that it will increase loyalty, patronage, and as much as possible, bring you new customers.

The community comprises of your customers and those who are not your customers. There are things you can do to ensure that you reach all these people. I have some suggestions below

Empowerment seminars

Is there an empowerment seminar coming up in your community? Call the organizers and ask them to tell you what you can do to help. They really would be glad to get associated with you. They will be glad that someone – "out of the blues" – has believed in them enough to want to identify with them. It is important to sponsor events like these since such events are always memorable because of the decisions and resolutions they will cause the participants to make. Whenever they see the outcome of the event, they will remember those who made it possible and that alone can bring about loyalty.

Youth party

A youth organization may be willing to hold a party for the young people in your community during Christmas,

Easter, or other celebrations. It is a good opportunity to be involved in sponsorship. Just a banner and a stand to serve free drinks and/or other freebies might be sufficient.

Boys' Scout and Red Cross

Organizations like the Boys' Scout and the Red Cross are globally known. They are known to train young people to be responsible and useful to themselves and to their communities. Sponsoring the local unit in your community will be a plus to your marketing efforts.

Women empowerment

In today's world of women rights and emancipation movement, especially in Africa, sponsoring an event for women empowerment will definitely be worthwhile. And don't forget that most buying decisions in the home are made by women.

Music/Comedy night

Music and comedy gets everyone's attention. Sponsoring a music or comedy event is a very good idea. In Lagos, most companies are more involved in sponsoring music and comedy than in any other singular social event.

The Freedom Example

What I call the Freedom example is what is done by Freedom Group of Companies in Benin City. They have business interests in solid minerals, beverages and so on. They made road signs all around the city. Some of them tell you that there is a bending ahead. Some inform you of a slope ahead. Other special ones identify the historic Benin Moats. Beneath each of these signs is written "freedom" in their brand colours.

Guaranty Trust Bank Plc has made this popular in many campuses and cities around the country. You too can do something like that in your community. And you can start small!

Scholarship

Why not award scholarship to someone? It could be that you will pay for someone's books, school fees, school pocket money or everything. You can publicize the selection process by involving the media.

Quiz Competition

You may want to encourage academic excellence by deciding to organize or sponsor a quiz competition for the schools in and around your host community. The prizes could include a scholarship, books, recreational materials, etc.

HOW TO BE INVOLVED IN EVENTS

We are more interested in the sponsorship of events because it is what people notice immediately. It can produce results both in the short and in the long term. How you want to be involved in sponsoring an event is dependent on how much you have (and I think it should be part of your marketing budget as your business grows bigger).

Cash donation: If you think you have enough funds to sponsor financially, you can do it. You may want to pay for the venue of the event, sponsor the printing of the promotional materials, pay for the decorations, or any form of rental. It is up to you.

Donation in kind: You can also donate in kind. Examples are donating a vehicle and a driver to be used during preparation for the event, donating personnel, lodging the speaker (or celebrities) if you are a hotel proprietor, and so on. The organizers will always enumerate all the areas in which they need sponsorship.

CAUTION
Fraudsters

Certain people may come to ask you to sponsor an event they know will never hold. Their aim is to get your hard-earned money and get lost. You have to be careful. One good way of knowing genuine people is to ask for proof of past events.

Your customer must benefit

Is the event for people who are your target customers? If it is not, you may not get the "customer approval" this kind of participation ought to get you. For example, a company that deals on sanitary pads for ladies may not get any benefit from sponsoring a football event for guys. They will, however, get 100% benefits from sponsoring an event that targets women as participants.

Know the details

What kind of event is it? Are the organizers hiding something? Is it an event you want to identify with? Is it one that your customers and other responsible people will like to associate with? Is the event going to be an orgy? Is it likely that someone would be raped at that event? Will you be promoting terrorism by sponsoring the event? You have to put all these and more unpleasant possibilities into consideration.

Know the terms

Ask for the terms of your involvement. Know them for sure and on paper. Where do you want your name to be on the materials and on the stage? What do you want to do at the venue? Would you want your sales people to storm the venue? Discuss the terms. Let the organizers know how you want to take advantage of whatever you are putting in for sponsorship to avoid confusion and strife.

As you have seen, being socially responsible is both exciting and profitable. Take advantage of it whenever the opportunity presents itself. It makes marketing sense!

Chapter 17

Online and Mobile Marketing

The Internet has over the years changed the way we live, work, do business, generate information, transfer information, broadcast and even the way we make and keep friends. I am an individual who has gained so much, especially in business, from the Internet. You probably got to know about this book on the internet. It is even possible you bought it online!

I have gained so much knowledge and experience since I first wrote this book and so much has changed. However, the basics as outlined in the entire book have not changed at all. This chapter was initially not a part of the book. I only just added it. I am very glad I didn't publish it before the advent of vigorous online and mobile marketing.

So, in the remaining part of this journey, I am going to show you how to get people to do business with you through the power of the Internet.

When I founded The Learning Edge Ltd alongside Blessing Odeh, we didn't stand a chance in commanding patronage or serious followership because apart from the fact that we didn't have much experience in consulting, training and recruitment then; we were faced by all the many challenges a startup would face. We didn't have enough capital to afford an office and all the many things we needed to operate smoothly. But we had one of the greatest business marketing tools in the world – Internet.

So, I began to utilize the Internet to the best of my ability and as I did, I learnt more and before we could say "Jack," our bank account was running in millions!

You can launch an Internet marketing program that is successful by concentrating your attention on the following

1. Email marketing
2. Social media
3. Blogging
4. Mobile marketing

Email marketing

You probably have read something about this before. Email marketing is a very powerful tool you can use to win customers.

What you need to start email marketing

1. Email addresses
2. A layout for the message if you want it to look like a newsletter
3. A landing page, should the receiver want to learn more

4. The content and format of your message

5. Customized reply for enquiries

6. A system that ensures that people are promptly replied

7. A telephone (preferably mobile) number by which you can be reached

8. A storage system for keeping details of enquirers and their enquiries

Let's have a brief discussion on the above

1. EMAIL ADDRESSES

The kind of people you want to reach with your message determines where you would source the email addresses. There are a number of ways you can get email addresses. When I first started, I got a little disappointed because I was getting only a handful from here and there. But you do not need to be. If you get a list of 50 people, be thankful because one day, you would get one of 500, 5000, 50000, etc.

How to get email addresses for a successful email campaign

1. **Ask**. Ask friends for help. Ask them to give you email addresses of the people in their offices, clubs, etc.

2. **Request for registration registers at events**. You may need to tip someone to make this happen.

3. **Download lists from the Internet**. Believe me; I have gotten several like this before. The most common ones are the committee members of various organizations.

4. **Facebook**. If you are patient enough to copy one email address after another, you can get thousands of email addresses on Facebook.

5. The contacts you have sent emails before.

Don't try to rush things. When I first started, it was tough but today, I have access to over 1, 000, 000 email addresses and the rate at which I now get new ones would take the number to over 2, 000, 000 soon. Patience is the key here.

2. LAYOUT FOR THE MESSAGE IF YOU WANT IT TO LOOK LIKE A NEWSLETTER

I am sure you have received e-newsletters at one point or the other before. Many organizations use the format of newsletters to send emails. The layout could be designed by you or your graphics person. The good news is that you do not even have to design anything. There are so many services you can use for FREE. Mailchimp, Campaign Monitor and Emma are arguably the 3 most popular services you can use. All you need to do is Google them and sign up on their websites. They have templates you can use. Like other e-marketing services, they have premium features you can subscribe for if you want to take your marketing to another level.

It is however not a rule to have a layout for your message. I have sent thousands of emails without using a layout. As long as your email is well formatted in such a way that no reader gets bored while reading, you are okay. I will show you how to format emails shortly.

3. A LANDING PAGE, SHOULD THE RECEIVER WANT TO LEARN MORE

Your letter has information for the reader. However, the letter alone may not be able to compel them to make a buying decision. This means that the message you have sent is just bait – something to entice the reader to want to *click to read more*.

The landing page is the page your prospect is taken to should he want to find out more information about your offer. It might be a page on your website, on your Facebook page, on your blog, etc.

One vital thing you must know while designing your landing page is to ensure that there is a form for your prospects to fill.

Why you need a form

As a good marketer, you want to get the information (phone number, email address, name and other particulars) of the people that visit your landing page. That is why you need a form on the page so you can carry out personal, one on one follow-up on them till they exchange their money for your offer.

4. THE CONTENT AND FORMAT OF YOUR MESSAGE

When sending emails in a marketing campaign, the content must be as short and simple as possible. That means you are supposed to say much with very few words. The best messages are those that personalize your message to the reader by use of words like "you", "your", etc. However, you would need to avoid words like 'I' in messages like these if you are writing on behalf of your company. Using "we" is best.

If you have much to say to your potential reader, itemize each point with bullets. The message should contain your phone number, email address and if you think it is necessary, include your office address. Then ensure the link to your landing page is very visible for your reader to know where to click to get more details.

In conclusion, remember to always keep it short and simple. And don't forget to edit your message over and over again for errors.

The more you do this, the more natural it will become to you.

5. CUSTOMIZED REPLY FOR ENQUIRIES

People are going to respond to your emails with enquiries. Even if they do not reply, they would fill your contact form. Prepare various messages that address the likely queries people would have. And then, modify the messages to suit each person. I have been doing this for many years now. In that way, even if I have as many as 30 enquiries, I am able to reply all of them within one hour! This message does not have to be as short as the marketing email. But ensure that you still communicate much with as little words as possible.

6. A SYSTEM THAT ENSURES THAT PEOPLE ARE PROMPTLY REPLIED

When I first started online marketing, I promised on our contact page that we would reply all enquiries within 12 hours. Later, I changed it to one hour! And I am going to keep changing it until I succeed in helping my businesses beat as many competitors as possible! I quoted Rupert Murdoch earlier in this book. He said that "the world is changing fast. Big will not beat small anymore. It will be the fast beating the slow." Reply enquiries as fast as possible!

7. **A TELEPHONE (PREFERABLY MOBILE) NUMBER BY WHICH YOU CAN BE REACHED**

I have already mentioned that you should have an email address, phone number and if possible, office address included in your marketing message. The importance of a phone number cannot be overemphasized.

The reason a phone number is important is that many people do not have the patience or the time to fill a contact form or send an email. If they have call credit, they want to get the information immediately.

When they call, explain in as simple terms as possible and still request for an email address so they can receive more details from you. And do not forget to keep records of the calls.

8. A STORAGE SYSTEM FOR KEEPING DETAILS OF ENQUIRERS AND THEIR ENQUIRIES

There should be software for this but I normally just use tables to organize prospects' information MS Word documents. I have various headings and filenames for them. For example, I have "January Advert Contacts", "Christmas Bonanza Contacts", etc. I have tried my hands on MS Excel but I am more comfortable with Word.

Your table should have the following fields – name, phone number, email, city and remark. Under remark, use a word or statement to summarize what the prospect wants and what has been done to help them.

You should always check this storage system and keep in close touch with your prospect until their details are moved to another table, "customers"!

Social Media Marketing

We started this chapter with Email Marketing. Let us now move on to Social Media Marketing. The social media offers businesspeople a unique opportunity to increase sales and visibility. So, as a businessperson or marketer, it is time to embrace the social network.

Of all the social media networks, Facebook has worked the most for me for the following reasons;

1. **Photos**: Facebook allows you to post photographs and gives you the opportunity of posting photographs of your business' activities. This increases credibility and serves as a tool to get more customers. Moreover, you can design fliers, convert them to jpeg format and post them as photographs. 'Tagging' people on your photographs also make the effect of the message

you send across to go viral because of the notification system facebook operates.

2. **Fan Pages**: Facebook pages allow you to get a special page with which you can promote your business on the social networking site. With fan pages, you can gather a lot of loyalty "followers" and build a stronger brand. Today, people tend to equate the strength of your brand to the number of "likes" your fan page gets. You can use this all important tool to move your business to the next level.

3. **Friends**: The first thing that makes Facebook very interesting is the fact that there are a lot of people and amongst these people are your friends and those who are capable of being your friends. This feature alone makes it a platform for everyone to be able to communicate with everyone else in their network of friends. This is so powerful. Imagine you have 5000 friends on Facebook. That means 5000 people primarily get to see whatever you say. What if you systematically do something that makes their

friends to be aware of what you said to them? Amazing!

4. **Acceptance**: The fact that close to every educated person has accepted Facebook and currently has an account on the platform makes your job of marketing on the platform rewarding.

Common mistakes people make with Facebook

1. **Taking their Facebook account too personal**: Some people take their facebook so personal to the point where they cannot use it to move their business forward.

2. **They see friends**: Is it possible to have up to 5000 friends in real life? I don't think so. However, Facebook makes it possible to! Many people do not accept friend request of people they do not know personally. Yet, they want their social media marketing to pay off. Personally, I do not see friends on Facebook. I see customers. So, I accept friend requests from every Tom, Dick and Harry because I know that

if they do not buy from me today, they would buy from me tomorrow.

3. **Their private life gets in the way**: Do not post too much personal information on a Facebook account you are supposed to be using for business. This is a fundamental mistake a lot of business people make. If your 'friends' on Facebook have learnt certain things about you, they might not be at liberty to do business with you.

4. **They expect to get everything free**: Yes, you can post photos and fliers on Facebook and get some patronage. However, you won't be able to make the kind of money you should be making if you ignore paying for advertisement. Put some money aside to make this happen. Facebook advertising is so cheap that you can even budget as little as $10 per day. As little as $200 can make strangers on Facebook notice what you do and buy from you.

There are plenty of resources available on Facebook that you can download to use for more information.

Other social networking websites you can use to promote your business include Linkedin, Twitter, Google+, etc.

People have approached me to ask if I can teach them how to use the social networking sites to grow their business. I always tell them that the best way to become proficient in getting results via the sites is by beginning to take steps. Start small. Don't expect to know everything in one day. As you watch what other people are doing and start doing them, you will start mastering newer things that other people have not known very well.

Blogging

Blogging can increase the number of business you get from time to time. Just one simple post can generate more enquiries than you can effectively manage. Blogging is very easy to start if you are new to it. Simply type blogging on google.com and you would get hundreds of articles that can help you to set up a blog, either on blogspot.com or on winepress.com.

Just one article on one of my blogs has generated over 5000 comments, some of which I have approved and some of which I have not had time to approve. Write things that concern your craft and post on your blog every day or week, depending on how much time you have. Then design linkable (or clickable) adverts and post them on the blog. This would increase traffic to your website or offers.

Important points to note

Customer service: No matter how good your marketing campaign is, you much ensure that the basic principles of customer service and satisfaction are well pursued. If this is missing, your online marketing campaign won't help you.

Promptness: I used to ensure that my businesses respond to customers' request in 12 hour at most. Recently I took it to 1 hour! Now, I am taking it to 30 minutes and very soon, it would be just 5 minutes. Promptness is the key to winning the customer's heart.

Follow-up: When you receive a prospect's details, it is important to start calling the prospect latest 3 days after the enquiry until he finally parts with the money and takes your product or service home.

Mobile marketing

For the benefit of our discourse, what I mean here is SMS Marketing. This kind of marketing takes advantage of the fact that almost everyone now has a mobile phone.

If you put an advertisement on TV or radio, chances that the message would get to the kind of persons it is intended for is far from 100%. There are many things that can make an individual not to see/hear a TV or radio advertisement.

1. He might be busy at the time of airing the advert
2. He might have visitors
3. He might be watching a movie

4. He might be watching a different channel

5. He might simply just dose off while the advert is on

However, if an individual gets a beep on his phone, his first instinct is to check and read whatever message he has received. Whether or not he contacts you, he has read your message. This makes SMS adverts more effective and measurable.

Characteristics of winning SMS

1. **It is short and simple**: Any Marketing SMS that is more than one page may not get the expected results because the message would show *missing message* until the remaining page(s) enter the person's phone. If the person's phone inbox is already full (as is the case many times), it takes a longer time. Your prospect ends up not getting the complete message at the time he should. The fact that people always put their contact details last can make the effort

defeated. It is always best to keep your message short and simple.

2. **It calls for action**: A winning marketing SMS must call for action. Your message must have "call now" or "register now" or some other form of call for action. Some people send messages and end them with their phone numbers. It is fine but it is more compelling if it says "call 0803####### now" or simply "call 0803#######"

3. **It is timely**: Your SMS would not get the expected results if they are sent at certain times of the day. I prefer to send SMS at the times I think people have reached their offices and settled down. I also send on Saturdays when people are either less busy or just relaxing after a long week. It depends on your city. Study it and know what works.

4. **It has a catchy sender ID**: The SMS that win always have a sender ID that is both relevant and interesting to the target customer. Avoid general taglines. Let your sender ID be unique.

The sender ID field on SMS service sites is always 11 characters. That gives you the opportunity to use your mobile phone number or an office phone number as the sender ID whenever you choose to.

5. **The SMS is sent in batches**: One of the things we always experience at my offices is that whenever we send SMS, we always have a lot of calls coming in at the same time. The "call waiting" setting makes it possible for us to see other calls coming in while we are answering an enquiry. Many times, if we do not pick up their calls, they may not call back. So, we started sending bulk SMS in batches. It takes more time and efforts but it pays off eventually. You don't want to send a message to 10000 phone numbers and end up receiving only 12 calls while others are being told that your number is busy or not reachable.

6. **No ambiguous languages – straight to the point**: Your message must be straight to the point. Avoid using ambiguous sentences. You

are not trying to impress. You want to sell! Let's keep it simple.

7. **They are sent to the right prospect**: You don't want to send bulk SMS and end up receiving phone calls from illiterates asking you to explain the message or asking if you have met somewhere before. You want to send your message to people who understand English language and are only calling for clarifications, cost, more details, etc. For this reason, you should get lists that contain the phone numbers of the kind of people you want to reach.

WHEN THEY CALL

Yes, people are going to call you when you send bulk SMS. How should you relate with them?

1. First of all, greet them and introduce yourself excitedly.

2. Ask for their name. For example, "My name is Kingsley. Who am I speaking with please?"

3. Give them all the necessary information they ask for.

4. Don't rush them but bear in mind that other people would at the same time be trying to reach you.

5. Have your answers handy.

6. Offer to send them an email that contains more details if they do not mind. Most times, they wouldn't. After all, email is cheaper than phone calls.

7. Ask them to send their email address via SMS. It is always more accurate compared to dictating it over the phone.

8. Ask if they are calling with their phone number. If they are not, politely ask for their phone number and write it down. Call that number back to confirm. Save their phone numbers.

9. It would be nice to ask them how they got to know about your company. After all, we all want to know where our money is coming from so that we can build up on it.

10. Invite them for a chat at your office if they want to. Otherwise, you may need to go to their office.

11. Save their details and promptly send more details to them.

12. Initiate a plan for follow up.

In summary, you would notice that Mobile Marketing is somewhat related to Online Marketing. SMS Marketing most times, is not enough. It gets complemented by emailing.

I wish you all the best in your marketing quest!

About the Author

Kingsley Aigbona started his career as the publisher of a monthly inspirational, motivational and personal development magazine. He is passionate about the development of individuals and has taught various audiences on goals, dream actualization, marketing and career development.

He is a contributor to The Unlikely Burden and Other Stories, a book which was the focus of a BBC analysis in October 2006. The book has been translated into Swahili, Portuguese and other languages and is widely distributed in East Africa and the Caribbean. He is also the author of How to Escape the Scourge of Unemployment, a book he distributes to NYSC Corp Members FREE OF CHARGE.

He is also one of the few individuals who were commissioned to write "How to Be A Good Lagosian" published for the Office of the Governor of Lagos State, Nigeria.

Kingsley Aigbona has a wealth of experience in marketing and leadership. He has worked as Business Development Manager at Mobile Rechargespot Limited, Marketing Manager at Supreme Option Technologies, and as Nigerian Coordinator of WSPA's Humane Education Programme.

Kingsley is a trained and practicing Public Relations practitioner and is certified by Nigerian Institute of Public Relations (NIPR). He is also a trained Humane Education Personnel by WSPA, UK.

He is currently the Head of Learning & Consulting at The Learning Edge Limited, a consulting, training and recruiting firm based in Lagos State, Nigeria. He has helped to design and organize courses that attract people from various organizations such as MTN, Visafone, Shell (Cameroun & Nigeria), SNEPCO, Guaranty Trust Bank Plc, Skye Bank Plc, ExxonMobil,

NLNG, Daewoo (Nigeria), NAFDAC, and more. He anchors strategy sessions, team bonding & induction activities for firms.

He has also trained for Ogun State House of Assembly, Masters Energy Oil & Gas Ltd, Basscomm Group, ASO Savings & Loans Plc, Bola Onadebanjo& Co, and more. He facilitates sessions on Workplace Mentoring, Workplace Attitude, Communication Skills, Leadership, Project Management, Conflict Management and other Workplace Activation courses.

Kingsley also currently serve as the Chief Executive Officer of Papa n Gold Group of Companies, a conglomerate that has interests in oil and gas, e-commerce, manufacturing, international trade to mention but a few.

For more information about Kingsley Aigbona visit

www.*kingsleyaigbona*.com

243

The Wow Factor Staff Workshops

Have you ever wondered why some people (who might not be as good as you) are always preferred by management when it comes to certain roles and benefits?

Have you wondered why certain people are like super stars in the workplace, liked by customers, coworkers and by management?

Why do the same people get sent for nice all-expense paid business trips?

Why do the same people get promoted every time there is an opening for one?

Why are some people so outstanding to the point that they are perceived as Workplace Superstars?

At The Wow Factor Staff Workshops, participants learn the secrets to becoming a Superstar at the workplace.

Call us today to book Kingsley Aigbona for your next training event.

+234 (0)8037368720, 8127706770

Effective Marketing Workshops

Do you want to increase your return on investment on marketing?

Call us to arrange a marketing training for your workforce.

Facilitated by Kingsley Aigbona and other experts, you will find the sessions practical, engaging, entertaining, educative and result oriented.

Call today or contact us via info@thelearningedge-ng.com. +234 (0)8037368720, 8127706770

Courses by The Learning Edge

The Learning Edge is a fast growing training and consulting organization which focuses on Learning and Development, Business Development, and Human Resource Management Services. Our passion to bring about significant change and increase in the performance of individuals and organizations has led to the provision of several business solutions and learning programs. The Learning Edge has trained the staff of many organizations in various industries such as banking, oil & gas, construction, manufacturing,

Our courses include but not limited to;

1. Professional Project Management
2. Customer Service Excellence Workshop
3. Events Design & Management

4. Effective Business Writing

5. Personal Effectiveness

6. Time Management

7. Effective Workplace Productivity Management

8. Change Management

9. Conflict Management

10. Effective Crisis Management

11. Accounting for Non-Financial Executives

12. Primavera for Technical & Non-technical Executives

13. Microsoft Project for Technical & Non-technical Executives

14. Teamwork Management

Call today or contact us via info@thelearningedge-ng.com.

+234 (0)8037368720, 8127706770